Escalation in the War in Ukraine

Lessons Learned and Risks
for the Future

BRYAN FREDERICK, MARK COZAD, ALEXANDRA STARK

T0308618

NATIONAL SECURITY RESEARCH DIVISION

For more information on this publication, visit **www.rand.org/t/RRA2807-1**.

About RAND

The RAND Corporation is a research organization that develops solutions to public policy challenges to help make communities throughout the world safer and more secure, healthier and more prosperous. RAND is nonprofit, nonpartisan, and committed to the public interest. To learn more about RAND, visit www.rand.org.

Research Integrity

Our mission to help improve policy and decisionmaking through research and analysis is enabled through our core values of quality and objectivity and our unwavering commitment to the highest level of integrity and ethical behavior. To help ensure our research and analysis are rigorous, objective, and nonpartisan, we subject our research publications to a robust and exacting quality-assurance process; avoid both the appearance and reality of financial and other conflicts of interest through staff training, project screening, and a policy of mandatory disclosure; and pursue transparency in our research engagements through our commitment to the open publication of our research findings and recommendations, disclosure of the source of funding of published research, and policies to ensure intellectual independence. For more information, visit www.rand.org/about/principles.

RAND's publications do not necessarily reflect the opinions of its research clients and sponsors.

Published by the RAND Corporation, Santa Monica, Calif.
© 2023 RAND Corporation
RAND® is a registered trademark.

Library of Congress Cataloging-in-Publication Data is available for this publication.

ISBN: 978-1-9774-1166-2

Cover image: Reuters.

About This Report

The ongoing Russian invasion of Ukraine has had devastating consequences, most notably for Ukraine itself but also for Russian military forces. Despite these costs, there appear to be several escalation options that the parties have refrained from undertaking. The most notable of these escalation options is Russian nuclear use, which has been threatened by Moscow but not undertaken.

This report evaluates the potential for further escalation in the conflict in Ukraine, including the prospects for escalation to Russian nuclear use. It does so by identifying and assessing the analytical mistakes made in both Russia and in the United States and other North Atlantic Treaty Organization (NATO) member states before the war, and how these shaped the behavior of all sides in the conflict to date. It then identifies potential future escalation options open to both Russia and Ukraine (including Russian nuclear use) and assesses the motivations, capacity to execute, and restraining factors likely to affect state decisions to pursue these options. The report is intended to (1) inform U.S. and NATO policymakers as they consider how to avoid further escalation of the conflict while assisting Ukraine in its efforts to defeat the Russian invasion and (2) better inform the public debate around these issues.

RAND Center for Analysis of U.S. Grand Strategy

This research was conducted within the RAND Center for Analysis of U.S. Grand Strategy. The center's mission is to inform the debate about the U.S. role in the world by more clearly specifying new approaches to U.S. grand strategy, evaluating the logic of different approaches, and identifying the trade-offs each option creates. Initial funding for the center was provided by a seed grant from the Stand Together Trust. Ongoing funding comes from RAND supporters and from foundations and philanthropists.

The center is an initiative of the International Security and Defense Policy Program of the RAND National Security Research Division (NSRD). NSRD conducts research and analysis for the Office of the Secretary of

Defense, the U.S. Intelligence Community, the U.S. State Department, allied foreign governments, and foundations.

For more information on the RAND Center for Analysis of U.S. Grand Strategy, see www.rand.org/nsrd/isdp/grand-strategy or contact the center director (contact information is provided on the webpage).

Acknowledgments

The authors wish to thank Miranda Priebe for providing essential guidance and invaluable feedback regarding the scoping and execution of the work. Mark Hvizda contributed valuable information regarding Russian actions in the conflict to date. The authors are deeply indebted to the participants of two brainstorming sessions, whose insights and expertise are reflected throughout this report. Several colleagues at RAND also provided helpful comments, including Raphael Cohen and Katya Migacheva. Daryl Press of Dartmouth College provided insightful feedback on an earlier draft of this report. Finally, the authors wish to thank several reviewers at RAND, including Heather Williams, who provided a thoughtful and thorough program review, and John Tefft (who has served as U.S. ambassador to several countries) and Alexis Blanc, who both provided peer reviews that greatly improved this document. All remaining errors or omissions are the responsibility of the authors alone.

Summary

Russia's ongoing invasion of Ukraine has the potential to lead to substantial further escalation, either inside Ukraine or in the potential for the conflict to expand to draw in other actors. In the extreme, the conflict offers plausible scenarios for Russia to become the first state to use nuclear weapons in warfare since 1945. Russia's decision calculus about conflict escalation was, not surprisingly, the focus of prewar analyses by the United States and the North Atlantic Treaty Organization (NATO). However, events since February 2022 have proven those analyses inaccurate or incomplete. Improving our understanding of what might prompt Russia or Ukraine to pursue escalation in this conflict and what might restrain them from doing so is therefore essential to better informing (1) decisions on how to reduce the risk of escalation while assisting Ukraine in its efforts to defeat the Russian invasion and (2) the public debate around these issues.

Approach

To better understand these issues, we convened two workshops in April 2023 and May 2023 made up of a diverse set of 15 experts with extensive experience focusing on Russia in and out of government, including experts working at the RAND Corporation and other nongovernmental and governmental organizations. These participants collectively have deep expertise in Russian leadership decisionmaking, military affairs, and nuclear weapons doctrine and capabilities. We supplemented these workshops with an extensive review of the policy and academic literature on both the present conflict and escalation dynamics more generally.

We focused on addressing two main sets of questions. First, what can we learn from the conflict to date about how Russia approaches escalation decisions? What has prompted Moscow to pursue escalation, and what has restrained them from doing so? Second, what escalation options do Russia and Ukraine have available to them in the conflict going forward? What would be the motivation of each state in pursuing such options, how practically capable of executing the option would they be, and what other factors would restrain them?

Key Findings

Any assessment of the risk of Russian escalation in the ongoing conflict in Ukraine should be approached with humility. Contrary to our prior estimates about how the Russian military would influence decisionmaking in a conflict, Russian President Vladimir Putin has adopted a more centralized, and apparently personalized, decisionmaking process. Even our estimates about Putin's future perceptions and reactions, based on Russian behavior in the Ukrainian conflict, should be tempered by the appreciation that Putin may be faced with circumstances and choices going forward that he has not previously faced. There are limits to what we can draw from the past to anticipate future Russian escalation decisions in such a personalized-driven process. That said, our research identified the following three main findings from assessing Russian behavior in the Ukrainian conflict:

- **Factors restraining Russian escalation.** Three main factors appear to have restrained Russian escalation in the conflict to date: (1) acute concerns for NATO military capabilities and reactions, (2) concern for broader international reactions, particularly the potential to lose support of the People's Republic of China, and (3) the Russian perception that its goals in Ukraine are achievable without further escalation, making riskier actions not yet necessary. However, different circumstances in the conflict, notably a dramatic change in the Russian battlefield position, a sharp deterioration in Russian internal stability, or a perception that NATO direct intervention is imminent or inevitable, could make these factors insufficient to restrain further deliberate Russian escalation.
- **Russian lack of preparedness for escalation.** Russia's lack of preparation and consideration of escalation options before the war appear to have made its approach to escalation in the conflict halting and incomplete. Russia dramatically overestimated its capabilities and prospects for success in its initial invasion while underestimating Ukrainian will

to resist and NATO cohesion. These factors meant that Russia devoted little effort before the war in planning for the contingencies it now faces and in developing viable escalatory courses of action.

- **Limited effectiveness of Russian escalation to date.** Moscow has pursued several escalatory measures in the conflict in a more ad hoc manner, including the shutoff of gas exports to Europe, the attempts to prevent Ukrainian grain shipments, and the expanded bombing campaign and human rights abuses against civilian targets inside Ukraine. These measures have tended to occur in conjunction with ongoing or anticipated Ukrainian offensives or battlefield success. However, none of these policies has altered Ukrainian or NATO behavior in the ways that Putin and his inner circle may have sought.

Regarding future risks of escalation in the conflict, we found the following:

- **Further deliberate escalation, including Russian nuclear escalation, is highly plausible.** Both Russia and Ukraine may still choose to deliberately escalate the conflict further. We identified six plausible options for Russian escalation that would have the potential to fundamentally alter the nature of the conflict, ranging from a limited attack on NATO to the use of chemical or nuclear weapons against Ukraine. We found that the most likely potential trigger for Russia to escalate the conflict is a perception that battlefield losses are threatening the security of its regime.
- **Fast-moving situations heighten escalation risks.** The speed with which Russian concerns for regime stability increase may play a critical role in determining the nature and likelihood of greater Russian escalation. For example, Russian battlefield losses that occur suddenly or unexpectedly, providing little time for reflection or the exploration of alternatives, would likely run a greater risk of escalation to nuclear use.
- **If it occurs at all, Russian nuclear use could be surprisingly extensive.** Should Russia decide to use nuclear weapons in the conflict, it may be relatively unrestrained in their employment. The Kremlin may assess that the costs and risks it would face from breaking the nuclear taboo would be similar regardless of whether a small or large number

of weapons were used or whether the warheads involved were tactical or strategic. Having decided to use these weapons, Moscow may decide, therefore, to use whatever number and size of weapons it deems are necessary to achieve its battlefield objectives.

- **Ukraine also has incentives to escalate.** Although Ukraine has been relatively constrained in its attacks on Russian territory to date, this pattern may not hold indefinitely because of both its own capability limitations and competing priorities and U.S. and NATO pressure to limit such attacks. Ukraine has strong motivations to strike inside Russia, including the desire to signal to the Russian public that there may be costs for continuing to support the conflict. Should Ukraine expand its attacks on sensitive targets inside Russia, and should those attacks increase in their effectiveness, these factors may increase Russian incentives to also consider more-escalatory options given the political risks for the Kremlin of appearing unable to prevent or respond to such attacks.

- **Inadvertent escalation risks persist.** In addition to these potential deliberate escalation pathways, the risk of inadvertent escalation in the ongoing conflict is likely to persist. Such escalation could occur as a result of the continued pursuit of military activities that are commonplace on both sides but happen to lead to different or unforeseen outcomes. The longer the conflict drags on, the more the risks of such circumstances occurring will accumulate.

Implications for U.S. and NATO Policymakers

This research highlights seven main implications for U.S. and NATO policymakers:

1. **NATO alliance cohesion is critical to managing escalation.** Maintaining NATO alliance cohesion regarding the escalation risks and how much risk to take on is a critical factor both in long-term Ukrainian military success and in helping to deter Russian horizontal escalation. Public disagreement within the Alliance regarding the

management of escalation risks could feed Russian perceptions that it can coerce NATO by threatening further escalation.

2. **NATO should prioritize maintaining consensus regarding support to Ukraine.** Decisions regarding the extent and pace of military support provided to Ukraine should reflect the importance of maintaining NATO cohesion on escalation management. Should the United States or another key NATO member decide to provide capabilities to Ukraine without consensus within the Alliance because of allied perceptions of the escalatory risk, and such disagreements became public, Russian perceptions that NATO would not respond in a unified, cohesive manner to escalation could strengthen.

3. **Range of military capabilities provided to Ukraine helps determine escalation risks.** Giving Kyiv the military capabilities to execute long-range strikes against sensitive targets inside Russia likely poses the greatest escalation risks. Particularly sensitive targets would include leadership, command and control, or politically important sites, such as Moscow. In addition to the operational or political value of such targets, Russia may view strikes on it as posing acute risks to the stability of the regime and be motivated to consider more-escalatory responses. Alternately, providing military capabilities with more limited range, whose utility would be constrained to attacks on Russian forces in Ukrainian territory, likely presents a lower level of escalatory risk.

4. **Trade-offs between supporting Ukraine and managing escalation may become more acute over time.** A more cautious, incremental approach to supporting Ukraine may require greater trade-offs to maintain in the future, depending on the trajectory of the conflict. If a planned summer 2023 Ukrainian counteroffensive falls short of its goals, for example, Western leaders could face a decision to either increase the technical capability and lethality of their support to Ukraine more quickly and dramatically or maintain a gradual approach to supporting Ukraine that limits at least some escalation risks but leaves open the possibility that Russia may eventually defeat Ukraine on the battlefield.

5. **Policymakers should be prepared to interrupt escalatory spirals from more-intensive Ukrainian attacks inside Russia.** If Russia

decides to unleash even more destructive attacks against Ukrainian civilian targets, an escalatory spiral could develop if Ukraine retaliates by conducting similar attacks, albeit likely at a smaller scale, inside Russia. Drone attacks against Moscow suggest the possibility of a future pattern of escalation in which both sides feel compelled to respond to or go beyond the most recent attacks. In this situation, the risks of vertical escalation are clear, but the risks of horizontal escalation against NATO may also become elevated as Russia gains increasing incentives to reduce Western support for Ukraine or prompt members of the Alliance to pressure Ukraine to cease its attacks. U.S. and NATO policymakers should prepare options to interrupt such escalation without undercutting Ukrainian battlefield objectives inside Ukraine.

6. **Effects of increasing Russian internal instability are difficult to predict.** Russian internal instability is likely to become an increasingly influential factor in Russian escalation decisions, though the direction of its effects is not yet clear. As the June 2023 Wagner mutiny highlights, the invasion of Ukraine has substantially eroded Russian state capacity, making the Kremlin's control of the country increasingly brittle. If the Kremlin believes that the demands of the Ukraine invasion are becoming too great for it to maintain internal order, it may be incentivized to explore possible partial withdrawals or ceasefire arrangements that allow for force reconstitution. However, faced with the same circumstances, the Kremlin could alternately conclude that, although it lacks the ability to sustain the conflict indefinitely, domestic pressure from hard-line, nationalist sources will not permit Russia to reduce its commitment to the invasion. This aspect would make escalatory options that shorten the conflict more appealing, including potentially nuclear use, even at the risk of possible NATO involvement or loss of support from China. How Putin will assess these varying risks to regime stability as they become more acute—and, therefore, the effects that they will likely have on Russian escalation decisions—is difficult to predict.

7. **Preparing for the failure of efforts to manage escalation, including to the nuclear level, is essential.** Finally, although preventing further escalation is a key objective of the United States and its allies

in the conflict, they should also plan for failure. Efforts to prevent or limit escalation may become increasingly difficult due to battlefield developments or Russian or Ukrainian decisions that are largely beyond the control of U.S. and European governments. Such escalation could plausibly include Russian nuclear use. This reality makes it necessary for U.S. and allied policymakers to robustly plan for how to respond to potential further Russian escalatory actions. It also highlights the value and importance of efforts to maintain political and military communication channels with Russia that could become vital to arrest an escalatory spiral.

Contents

Figures and Table

Figures

Table

CHAPTER 1

Introduction

Objective and Background

Despite the devastating losses experienced by the Russian military and both the Ukrainian military and civilian population following Russia's February 2022 invasion of Ukraine, both sides have refrained from pursuing several escalatory options to date. Although Russia particularly has escalated its attacks on Ukraine in several ways since the start of the invasion, it has refrained from other options—notable given the high stakes for the Kremlin and the potential capabilities Russia could bring to bear in the conflict. For example, Russian President Vladimir Putin has chosen not to escalate the conflict horizontally by attacking the United States or other members of the North Atlantic Treaty Organization (NATO) for their support to Ukraine and punishment of Russia. Moscow has also avoided certain vertical escalation options against Ukraine, most notably nuclear use, although it has pursued others, such as the expansion of its long-range strike campaign against Ukrainian critical infrastructure targets.

If Russian territorial, personnel, and materiel losses continue to mount without improvements on the battlefield, however, Putin will face a host of unpalatable options: negotiations from a position of weakness, more-extensive and potentially destabilizing mobilizations, or more draconian attempts to ensure internal control, among others. Putin's avoidance of certain escalatory options thus far does not preclude significant escalation, including nuclear escalation, in the future, particularly if Russia's fortunes continue to decline. Left with the prospect of mounting costs and losses, Putin and his political allies may come to see further escalation, despite its risks, as preferable to other options.

Our report explores three main questions. First, what can we learn from Russia's behavior to date about the risks of escalation in the present conflict? Second, what trajectories might the war take that could increase Russia's willingness to escalate, particularly regarding nuclear use? Third, what lessons can we draw that may help inform decisions by U.S. and NATO policymakers, both in the current conflict and in future conflicts involving nuclear powers?

Research Approach

Our efforts to address these questions combined extensive review and discussion of prior literature on escalation, both in this conflict and more broadly, and two structured brainstorming sessions. These brainstorming sessions included a total of 15 experts with extensive experience focusing on Russia in and out of government, including experts working at RAND and other nongovernmental and governmental organizations, and deep expertise in Russian leadership decisionmaking, military affairs, and nuclear weapons doctrine and capabilities.[1] In these brainstorming sessions, we asked the participants to respond to two main sets of questions:

- First, we asked these experts to identify past assumptions about Russia's willingness to escalate and reconsider Russian decisionmaking about escalation in light of Russia's wartime behavior. These experts examined previous assumptions, prominent factors involved in Russia's decisions to date to avoid escalation with NATO or nuclear escalation against Ukraine, and possible discontinuities between earlier periods in the war and Russia's current situation. The experts were then asked to identify the extent to which Russia's escalation decisions to this point in the war have either confirmed or disproven those assumptions.

---

[1]   All quotes in this report, unless otherwise noted, are drawn from these brainstorming sessions conducted in person with these 15 experts in Arlington, Virginia, in April 2023 and May 2023.

- Second, we asked these experts to outline Russia's assessment of its current situation, potential decision points for future escalation based on these assessments of the war's trajectory, and the tools for escalation available to Russia's leaders.

The insights gained from these brainstorming sessions enabled our expert groups to identify a set of most plausible and most concerning pathways to escalation in light of Russian leaders' assessments of the situation and tools that remain available to them. As noted, we supplemented these brainstorming sessions with an extensive review of the academic and policy literature on escalation dynamics, particularly as these texts relate to conflicts involving nuclear powers, which is summarized below.

We further relied on inputs from both the brainstorming sessions and the literature reviews to improve our understanding of the risks and dynamics of escalation for future conflicts involving nuclear powers more generally. This was a particular focus because Russia's behavior to date could lead policymakers to conclude that because Moscow has done less to escalate than previously believed in the conflict thus far, it would remain less likely to do so in the future. In turn, this conclusion could lead to a false sense of security in this or future conflicts or crises. Therefore, we offer conclusions and recommendations that may be helpful for understanding escalation management with nuclear-armed states in future conflicts.

Defining Escalation

We define *escalation* as an increase in the intensity or scope of a militarized crisis or conflict "that crosses threshold(s) considered significant by one or more of the participants."[2] We consider the possibility of both vertical escalation (i.e., changes in the intensity of conflict) and horizontal escalation (i.e., changes in the geographic scope of conflict) and mechanisms by

---

[2] Forrest E. Morgan, Karl P. Mueller, Evan S. Medeiros, Kevin L. Pollpeter, and Roger Cliff, *Dangerous Thresholds: Managing Escalation in the 21st Century*, RAND Corporation, MG-614-AF, 2008, p. xi; Alex Braithwaite and Douglas Lemke, "Unpacking Escalation," *Conflict Management and Peace Science*, Vol. 28, No. 2, April 2011.

which escalation might occur: deliberate, inadvertent, or accidental. Each of these three mechanisms is explained later in this chapter.

In this report, we focus on escalation in the conflict after the beginning of the Russian invasion in February 2022 and escalation efforts that might occur going forward. Although this conflict is primarily between Russia and Ukraine, many of the future escalation pathways discussed in this report fundamentally concern the potential for conflict between Russia and NATO (particularly the United States). This concern is the case for horizontal escalation risks that might involve direct conflict between Russia and NATO, but vertical escalation risks against Ukraine may also increase the risk of more direct NATO involvement, for example in response to Russian nuclear use against Ukraine. Therefore, the literature we review below primarily focuses on escalation between nuclear powers to best provide context for these dynamics.

It is worth noting, however, that the Russian decision to invade Ukraine in 2022 also reflected a decision to dramatically escalate a long-running conflict with Ukraine specifically, ongoing since at least 2014. Although not the focus of this report, the Russian decision to escalate that long-running conflict by undertaking the February 2022 invasion does reflect dynamics highlighted in academic research. For example, scholars have explored why the efforts of stronger states to coerce weaker states are often unsuccessful and found that stronger states tend to underestimate the incentives of weaker states to avoid developing a reputation for giving in to such coercion.[3] The coercive effects of nuclear-armed states against non-nuclear-armed states have also been analyzed and found to be no more effective than coercive efforts by states without nuclear weapons because of the challenges of making nuclear threats credible, given the extensive costs perceived likely to accompany their use.[4] Such research provides important insights into the challenges Russia faced in its efforts to coerce a change in Ukrainian behavior in the lead-up to the invasion, compounded by the fact that Ukrainian officials and the Ukrainian public appear to have believed until just before-

---

[3] Todd S. Sechser, "Goliath's Curse: Coercive Threats and Asymmetric Power," *International Organization*, Vol. 64, No. 4, Fall 2010.

[4] Todd S. Sechser and Matthew Fuhrmann, "Crisis Bargaining and Nuclear Blackmail," *International Organization*, Vol. 67, No. 1, Winter 2013.

hand that the threat of invasion was a bluff, despite extensive evidence to the contrary provided by U.S. intelligence agencies.[5] This literature also reflects relevant considerations for future escalation pathways that relate solely or primarily to Russia and Ukraine.

However, the escalation pathways of greatest concern to U.S. and NATO policymakers going forward involve the risk of conflict between Russia and NATO, either implicitly or explicitly. As noted above, such risks may occur either deliberately, inadvertently, or accidentally.

Deliberate Escalation

Deliberate escalation occurs when one side escalates purposefully to prevent defeat or gain an operational advantage. If a cataclysmic outcome (such as nuclear retaliation or significant territorial loss) appears to be inevitable, states may have a greater incentive to escalate first. This incentive is sharpened when a state believes that there is a limited window of opportunity, or temporary chance to avert disaster, by striking first.[6]

The potential for states to deliberately escalate to nuclear use deserves special consideration. Strategists have theorized two main circumstances in which deliberate nuclear escalation may be possible. The first of these may occur if a state believes that its capability to assure the destruction of its adversary in the event of a nuclear exchange has eroded, a condition known as crisis instability.[7] In his 1960 book *The Strategy of Conflict*, Thomas Schelling writes that although the initial probability of a state desiring to launch a first strike is small, the "initial probabilities of surprise attack become larger—may generate a 'multiplier' effect—as a result of [the] compounding of each person's fear of what the other fears."[8] In other words, if one side believes that the other is likely to escalate to nuclear use and launch

---

[5] Amy Mackinnon and Mary Yang, "Ukraine Urges the West to Chill Out," *Foreign Policy*, January 28, 2022; Mansur Mirovalev, "Why Most Ukrainians Don't Believe Biden's Warnings, Distrust West," *Al Jazeera*, February 21, 2022.

[6] Morgan et al., 2008.

[7] Elbridge A. Colby and Michael S. Gerson, eds., *Strategic Stability: Contending Interpretations*, U.S. Army War College Press, February 2013.

[8] Thomas Schelling, *The Strategy of Conflict*, Harvard University Press, 1960, p. 208.

a strike, that state's own incentive to strike first increases, particularly if it feels that its own retaliatory ability may be compromised. It should be noted that others have argued that Schelling's model is too narrowly focused on potential first-strike advantages. "By itself," Robert Powell argues, "the existence of [a first-strike advantage] is not enough to create instability."[9] This is also borne out by historical examples: In both the 1940s Berlin Blockade and the 1962 Cuban Missile Crisis, Powell argues, U.S. leaders did not demonstrate significant concern about the prospect of a Soviet nuclear first strike.[10]

The second set of circumstances under which deliberate nuclear escalation may occur is when a state assesses that battlefield conditions appear to be creating unacceptable political risks or outcomes, including the possibility of regime collapse or overthrow.[11] Under such circumstances, a state may decide to use nuclear weapons to coerce its opponent into a accepting ceasefire that averts these acute battlefield risks by forcing the other state to choose between a ceasefire that may limit its gains and a continuation of the conflict that might involve nuclear use against its own territory.

Beyond these two sets of circumstances, it is important to note that, as Reid Pauly and Rose McDermott argue, although traditional formulations of nuclear brinkmanship are framed in rational terms, human emotion and psychology are also a source of risk during a nuclear crisis.[12] In short, "in a MAD [mutually assured destruction] world, it is irrational to carry out a nuclear threat if massive nuclear retaliation is expected; but a human deci-

---

[9]   Robert Powell, "Crisis Stability in the Nuclear Age," *American Political Science Review*, Vol. 83, No. 1, March 1989, p. 62; Reid B. C. Pauly and Rose McDermott, "The Psychology of Nuclear Brinksmanship," *International Security*, Vol. 47, No. 3, Winter 2022–2023, p. 16; Robert Powell, "The Theoretical Foundations of Strategic Nuclear Deterrence," *Political Science Quarterly*, Vol. 100, No. 1, Spring 1985.

[10]   Powell, 1989, p. 72; Richard K. Betts, *Nuclear Blackmail and Nuclear Balance*, Brookings Institution Press, 1987, p. 164.

[11]   Keir A. Lieber and Daryl G. Press, *Coercive Nuclear Campaigns in the 21st Century: Understanding Adversary Incentives and Options for Nuclear Escalation*, Project on Advanced Systems and Concepts for Countering Weapons of Mass Destruction, Report No. 2013-001, March 2013; Brad Roberts, "NATO's Nuclear Deterrent: Fit for Purpose?" *SIRIUS Zeitschrift für strategische Analysen*, March 2023.

[12]   Pauly and McDermott, 2022–2023, p. 13.

sionmaker acting on emotion or psychological bias might do so anyway."[13] In the high-stress situation of a nuclear crisis, people may not always act like "rational" actors. Psychological biases can also heighten escalation risk: For example, leaders tend to overestimate the organization and unity of the other side and tend to see themselves as having more control over the outcomes of a system than they actually do ("illusion of control").[14] Humans can also simply lose self-control in a high-risk situation, making decisions guided by such emotions as a desire for revenge, pride, or status-seeking.[15]

Inadvertent Escalation

Conflicts can also escalate without a deliberate, premeditated decision by either side. In inadvertent escalation, one side takes an action that it does not perceive as escalatory but that its opponent interprets as such.[16] For example, in his book *Inadvertent Escalation*, Barry Posen demonstrates how large-scale conventional operations could interact with an adversary's nuclear forces and inadvertently degrade their second-strike capabilities.[17] A direct conventional attack on an opponents' nuclear forces, on command and control systems, "or even attacks on general-purpose forces that protect strategic nuclear forces," could lead to "heightened preparations for nuclear operations" or even a "response that actually employed nuclear weapons, ranging from limited demonstrative or tactical employment, through large-scale theater attacks, to full-scale counterforce exchanges."[18]

This dynamic represents a version of the security dilemma, in which operations designed to gain a conventional advantage have the unintended effect of making the other side's second-strike capabilities more vulnerable. The threatened party's harsh reaction to such an attack is, in turn, miscon-

---

[13] Pauly and McDermott, 2022–2023, p. 9.

[14] Pauly and McDermott, 2022–2023, pp. 30–31.

[15] Pauly and McDermott, 2022–2023, p. 33.

[16] Morgan et al., 2008, pp. 23–25.

[17] Barry R. Posen, *Inadvertent Escalation: Conventional War and Nuclear Risks*, Cornell University Press, 1991.

[18] Posen, 1991, pp. 3–4.

strued by the first side as evidence of malign intent rather than as a defensive reaction. Posen outlines a hypothetical example set in the late Cold War period: During a conventional war in Europe between the Warsaw Pact and NATO, "large-scale military engagements near or over the Soviet Union . . . could be (or be perceived to be) threatening Soviet strategic nuclear forces. Commanders of Soviet strategic forces may fear that surprise nuclear attacks could be camouflaged by the confusion . . . of intense conventional combat."[19]

Inadvertent escalation may be more difficult to deter because it is not the result of an intentional decision to pursue escalation by the adversary. However, other mechanisms can prevent inadvertent escalation, including making a conscious effort by decisionmakers to recognize potential pathways for inadvertent escalation before a conflict begins (e.g., by analyzing intelligence about an adversary's behavior and capabilities and assessing one's own actions with an eye to how one's actions could be perceived as escalatory) and making decisionmakers aware of the possibility of inadvertent escalation.[20] These mechanisms could also involve warning adversaries about the risks they may not recognize, although this warning may pose a dilemma if decisionmakers are unwilling to admit deficiencies in their own side's capabilities to the adversary.[21]

Accidental Escalation

Finally, accidental escalation may occur as the result of an unintended action or mistake (in contrast with inadvertent escalation, in which the action is intended).[22] Examples could include the accidental discharge of a weapon or mechanical failure leading to the crash of an aircraft that is then misinterpreted. Accidental escalation may also occur if military forces take actions that were not intended by leaders, either by accident or on purpose. During the 1962 Cuban Missile Crisis, for example, U.S. military operations were

---

[19] Posen, 1991, p. 15.

[20] Morgan et al., 2008, p. 25.

[21] Posen, 1991, pp. 24–25.

[22] Scott D. Sagan, *The Limits of Safety: Organizations, Accidents, and Nuclear Weapons*, Princeton University Press, 1993; Morgan, 2008, p. 165.

conducted according to standard operating procedures with which senior leaders were unfamiliar, meaning that these leaders did not fully understand the specific rules of engagement that would be followed in the execution of their orders.[23] Accidental escalation could occur when someone who is not the leader designated to make such a decision takes actions with escalatory effect—for example, in a system in which military commanders have been pre-delegated authorities by national leaders.[24]

Report Organization

This report is divided into four chapters, including this introduction (Chapter 1). Chapter 2 examines what we have learned so far about Russia's escalation decisionmaking from ongoing conflict in Ukraine. It also identifies the extent to which prewar beliefs were borne out by Russia's behavior in the war to date. Chapter 3 examines the risk of escalation in the ongoing war, including both inadvertent and deliberate escalation possibilities. It identifies likely future decision points for escalation, the tools that Russia (and, to a much lesser extent, Ukraine) has for escalation, and Russia's escalation options. Chapter 4 concludes by identifying the lessons from previous chapters for future conflicts and summarizing resulting policy recommendations.

---

[23] Morgan, 2008, p. 27; Graham T. Allison, *Essence of Decision: Explaining the Cuban Missile Crisis*, Little, Brown and Company, 1971.

[24] Pauly and McDermott, 2022–2023, p. 45.

CHAPTER 2

Learning About Russian Escalation Decisions from the Conflict

One of the key drivers in U.S. policy decisions regarding support for Ukraine has been an intense focus on the potential consequences of that support, particularly in terms of escalatory responses from Russia. With the war well into its second year, many early decisions to initially withhold capabilities from Ukraine, such as artillery, main battle tanks, long-range strike systems, and fighter aircraft have ultimately been modified or reversed outright. Many systems that previously raised grave questions about what Russia's response might be are now key parts of Ukraine's military operations. Despite this aspect and Ukraine's international supporters' continued military aid, NATO governments remain wary of the consequences of this support. In short, a key question for many of these governments remains centered on where Russia's redlines might be for further escalation.

It would appear that U.S. analysts predicted a much greater willingness on Russia's part to escalate than what Russian decisionmakers—most notably Putin—have been willing to tolerate under these circumstances based on Russia's actions to this point in the war. It is less clear what should be learned from these errors for the future. In particular, any assumption that the observed Russian hesitancy to escalate further will continue regardless of circumstances may fail to account for a variety of factors that could change, including Russian leadership perceptions of Russia's strategic success and failure, elite opinion, political resilience and internal stability, and sudden irreparable battlefield losses, among many others. The conflict has provided substantial information regarding what Western analysts got wrong before the war. But what has been learned should not necessarily make us more confident about our ability to better anticipate Russian escalation decisions going forward, as many of the key factors in these decisions reflect perceptions and calculations in the mind of Putin, about which we have limited information.

Lessons Learned About Russian Escalation Decisions

Prior to the Russian invasion of Ukraine, U.S. policymakers and analysts appear to have been operating on a set of assumptions about how and why Russia would consider escalation that has proven to be inaccurate, or at least incomplete. Broadly speaking, these misjudgments appear to have been due to two interrelated factors. First, outside actors appear to have misunderstood how strategic decisions are in practice made in Russia and specifically how poor information and decisionmaking processes can lead to choices, including regarding when and how to escalate, that differ from what would be expected to advance Russian interests. Second, there appears to have been a substantial misreading of Russian risk tolerance and willingness to militarily confront NATO on such interests as Ukraine that are strategically vital to Russia. As one expert pointed out, Putin was treated "as a rational thinker with good information." In reality, Putin overemphasized secrecy in planning the invasion, overestimated the quality of his plan and prospects for success, and underestimated both Ukrainian will and Western cohesiveness. These pathologies have persisted throughout the conflict and are likely an important factor in explaining Russian escalation decisions to date.

What Putin Got Wrong

President Putin has proven to be wrong on many fronts in his assessment of the conflict, often in ways that confounded Western analysts who previously viewed him as a strategic thinker, bold decisionmaker, and adept planner. As many of our expert panelists pointed out during our brainstorming sessions, Putin's miscalculations created situations for which he and his closest advisers were unprepared. This unpreparedness most likely caught Russia's leaders flatfooted and searching for solutions to several unforeseen problems. Most notably, several of our experts argued that these missteps may well have contributed to Russia's approach to escalation in the conflict.

Strategic Misjudgment and Poor Invasion Planning

Prior to the war, Russia's leaders considered escalation scenarios involving a potential Ukraine conflict to involve two distinct problems: one oriented toward Ukraine itself and the other focused on deterring NATO intervention. On the latter front, Russian efforts were successful in deterring direct NATO intervention. Although the United States engaged in a pronounced diplomatic and information campaign to illuminate Russian plans for invasion in advance and discourage Moscow from invading, the prospects of a potential nuclear conflict with Russia encouraged NATO leaders to explicitly rule out in advance any potential direct intervention to defend Ukraine, a policy that continues to date. But potential escalation dynamics with Ukraine itself, or possible longer-term escalation risks involving NATO should the conflict drag on, appear not to have been considered.

Russian leaders—as demonstrated in the Russian military's planning and preparations—assumed the war would be over quickly. For this reason, Putin and his close advisers did not anticipate the escalation decisions they would face as their invasion of Ukraine stalled and became protracted. At most, our experts contended that Russia possibly anticipated Ukraine would engage in unconventional warfare and considered how to respond but was unprepared for effective military resistance on a national scale, facilitated by the eventual level of NATO support that materialized. Therefore, the Russian leadership does not appear to have thought in advance about how it would approach vertical escalation decisions toward Ukraine, as it assessed that the campaign was likely to be successful in its initial phase.

This confidence in rapid Russian military victory is also critical in explaining why U.S. efforts to discourage Russia from invading Ukraine in February 2022 were ineffective. Having assessed that Russian forces would be able to seize Kyiv quickly, any NATO promises to provide Ukraine with substantial, sustained military assistance would likely have been treated as essentially irrelevant to the initial Russian goal to "denazi" the government of Ukrainian President Volodymyr Zelenskyy.[1] Once key NATO countries (particularly, the United States) explicitly ruled out direct intervention in the conflict, the Russian decision to invade then appeared in Moscow to be a question of balancing the strategic gains of assured battlefield success against the prospect of longer-term economic or diplomatic consequences. Russia likely discounted even the effects of these nonmilitary levers as a result of Moscow's perception that NATO cohesion and support for Ukraine would be unlikely to be sustained.

In this regard, Russia singularly failed to appreciate the effect that its prosecution of the war would have on allied governments and publics in NATO, especially among European NATO members. Although NATO cohesion may have appeared mixed in the months and weeks preceding the invasion, in part because of varied reactions to declassified U.S. intelligence assessments that Russia was planning to invade, Russia's brazen invasion and subsequent brutal prosecution of the campaign helped to manufacture a sea change in European political and strategic calculations toward Russia that has proven to be an essential factor in sustaining support for Ukraine throughout the lengthy war. This sharply more adversarial attitude toward Moscow in many NATO countries has also given rise to additional escalation risks for Russia that do not appear to have been anticipated.

One the most significant oversights in Russian planning, according to our expert panels, was that Russia's leaders did not anticipate the extent to which escalation dynamics with NATO and Ukraine would become entangled as NATO assistance to Ukraine became a crucial factor in the war. Even following early setbacks, including the Russian inability to take Kyiv, many Russian senior leaders likely felt they were winning and that NATO involvement would not be a decisive factor in the war. Similarly, NATO signaled its own desire to avoid conflict by withdrawing U.S. personnel from Ukraine. However, as NATO assistance to Ukraine began to become a crucial factor in both sustaining and expanding Ukrainian military capabilities, Russia appears to have been uncertain how to deter NATO from providing this assistance.

---

[1]   Rachel Treisman, "Putin's Claim of Fighting Against Ukraine 'Neo-Nazis' Distorts History, Scholars Say," NPR, March 1, 2022.

Ultimately, Russia's initial view of escalation dynamics with Ukraine and NATO as being separate issues presented a conundrum for Russian leaders. As NATO support continued to grow incrementally and have a more significant effect on the conflict, Russian leaders were hesitant to pursue some escalatory options for fear of provoking direct NATO intervention. As one panel expert concluded, Russia is "genuinely afraid of NATO, it's not just posturing" and Russian officials "know it is possible to put the U.S. leadership in a position where [it] might attack." On the other hand, Russia has been much more willing to pursue escalation against Ukraine when it did not assess NATO direct intervention in response to be likely. However, these efforts have generally not been successful in shifting the course of the war due in large part to the Kremlin's misreading of Ukrainian will to fight. To this point, Russia's attempts at vertical escalation, such as the expansion of missile strikes against Ukrainian critical infrastructure in fall 2022, have been highly destructive but have fallen short of their intended objectives. Instead, they have hardened Ukrainian resolve and led to calls for increased Western support.

Misperceptions About Ukrainian Capabilities and Will to Fight

Another key factor that likely affected Russia's consideration of more-escalatory approaches has been, according to one brainstorming session participant, its "complete misperception of Ukrainian motivations and will to fight." It appears that, in planning the 2022 invasion of Ukraine, the Russian leadership's perception of the ease with which Russian forces seized Crimea in 2014 shaped Moscow's understanding of how the 2022 war would likely unfold. As several experts argued, Crimea was the seminal experience for both Russian Defense Minister Sergei Shoigu and Russian Chief of the General Staff Valery Gerasimov and almost certainly informed their assumptions about Ukraine's will to fight and ability to resist prior to the invasion. In addition, a decade of military reforms, major investments, and successful operations in Crimea and Syria most likely led Russian leaders to be confident in Russian military capabilities relative to Ukraine's.

Russia's overconfidence in its capabilities was accompanied by a gross misreading of Ukrainian motivations and will to fight. At the macro level, Russia fundamentally missed the shift in Ukrainian civic identify that occurred over the 2014–2022 period. Russia's assessment of Zelenskyy and his election was a significant part of this misperception. Putin and his inner circle saw Zelenskyy as the peace candidate and ultimately not a serious leader who could stand up to Russia. This gave Russian leaders a false sense of confidence that Ukraine was the same corrupt, leaderless entity that they encountered in early 2014.

These perceptions missed the mark in two critical areas that would have a major impact on the success of Russia's war plan and the impact of its early attempts to escalate against Ukraine. First, Russian assessments completely missed the progress in Ukraine's development of democratic political institutions and a cohesive national identity that took place over the previous eight years. These developments provided a psychological foundation for Ukraine's will to resist after the invasion began. Russia's planning also incorrectly assumed Ukraine's leadership was corrupt at all levels of the state and could be co-opted, thereby diminishing the effectiveness of Ukraine's resistance. Second, investments in Ukraine's military capabilities in the eight years following Crimea were greatly underappreciated by Russia's leadership. These investments included an increasingly close relationship with the United States that provided both weapons and training. This relationship built important connections that opened avenues for support early on following the invasion and permitted a conduit for the United States and its European partners and allies to gradually build support for Ukraine's military. These misperceptions likely led Russia to conclude that planning for further escalatory measures was unnecessary in the early stages of the conflict. When battlefield reversals could not be denied by the end of summer 2022, Russia began to adopt an escalation strategy—in particular, the expanded critical infrastructure campaign—the success of which was predicated on the same negative assessments of Ukrainian resolve that sabotaged the effectiveness of the initial Russian campaign.

Misperceptions About European Politics and Western Unity

Russia's incorrect assessments of Western resolve and unity also proved to be a major misjudgment that had a significant impact on Russia's escalation calculus. According to one of our panelists, "Russians still suffer from misconceptions about European politics and unity"—a problem that "causes them to reduce their assessments of the risks/costs they run" when confronting Europe. In part, these misperceptions also carried over to Russia's views on U.S. willingness to intervene or support Ukraine. As mentioned in the previous section, Russia's key leaders were shaped by their experiences in 2014—a conflict in which neither the United States nor its allies and partners chose to intervene. U.S. statements prior to the 2022 conflict in Ukraine demonstrated a clear desire on the part of Western nations to avoid escalation by not directly intervening in Ukraine to counter the Russian invasion. Putin's personal assessments of U.S. and European leadership also likely played a significant role in shaping these misperceptions, particularly following the 2021 departure of German Chancellor Angela Merkel from politics and the U.S. pullout from Afghanistan. Both events, among others, appear to have been interpreted by the Russian leadership as evidence that U.S. and European leadership was weak.[2]

From the outset of the war, Russia's strategy involved a belief that the Western alliance could be fractured if the appropriate threats and pressure were applied. What Russia's leaders found, however, was a Western alliance that found support from other major democratic powers and remained unified in its approach to sanctions and in providing both lethal and nonlethal support to Ukraine. More specifically, the widespread NATO willingness to support Finland's and Sweden's admittance to the Alliance demonstrated a sense of unity that Russia had not anticipated. Similarly, European energy policies and willingness to seek alternative sources of fuel demonstrated that Russia had greatly overestimated its leverage over Western Europe. As noted earlier, Russia's misunderstanding of Western cohesion was likely both a misperception of the latent degree of allied political and diplomatic unity and a total failure to recognize how that unity would be enhanced by the experience of observing Russia's brutal conduct in the war. These misperceptions likely affected Russia's approach to horizontal escalation, specifically its apparent misperception that escalatory threats and economic pressure alone could alter U.S. and European behavior and weaken support for Ukraine over time. Instead, the opposite has proven to be the case.

---

[2]   Andrew Osborn, "Senior Russian Security Official Questions U.S. Commitment to Ukraine After Afghan Exit," Reuters, August 19, 2021.

Summary

Russia has pursued escalatory options in its invasion of Ukraine, ranging from its cutoff of gas deliveries to Europe to the expansion of its bombing campaign against Ukrainian infrastructure and civilian targets, but it has miscalculated their effectiveness due to its persistent misperceptions about U.S. and European resolve, NATO willingness to provide material aid to Ukraine, and Ukrainians' will to fight. In terms of economic warfare, one expert on our panel pointed out that "Russia may have thought that winter would solve the problem of Western support." However, because of a combination of favorable weather and policies in Western Europe that mitigated the effect of Russia's energy embargoes, these attempts to undermine public support for NATO's efforts to support Ukraine fell well short of their intended goal. Likewise, limited nuclear signaling and generalized threats of future retaliation did little to instill fear in the vast majority of allied populations. Inside Ukraine, Russia's attempts to escalate the conflict by destroying critical infrastructure and targeting civilian population centers also proved ineffective in eroding Ukraine's willingness to resist Russian aggression.

Western Prewar Expectations and Assessments

Russia's behavior in the conflict has confounded Western observers on many levels. Analysts who had watched the Russian military train, read its doctrinal writings, and observed its military operations since 2014 were shocked by the poor planning, incompetence, and unreliability that marked the initial phases of the invasion. Few, if any, longtime observers—even those who suspected critical shortfalls in Russia's military capability—anticipated such a poor showing. Likewise, many Western analysts expected Russia's leadership to be much more aggressive toward NATO and much more willing to escalate to prevent NATO's intervention in the conflict, even indirect involvement, such as providing support to Ukraine. As one expert involved in the brainstorming sessions noted, "We overestimated their willingness to escalate in red teaming," and Russia's "actual fear of NATO is likely more acute."

Understanding how and why the West was mistaken in understanding Russian behavior is important for anticipating the potential risks of escalation in the conflict going forward. For example, NATO member states clearly underestimated the scale of military assistance that could be provided to Ukraine without triggering a Russian escalation against NATO in this conflict. But this fact does not necessarily mean that future or expanded assistance will not contribute to Russian escalation under different circumstances. Therefore, a better understanding of why Russia has limited horizontal escalation to date is critical. Next, we summarize three key types of mistaken prewar expectations and assessments with implications for the future.

Russian Tolerance of NATO Assistance to Ukraine

The gradual buildup of military support for Ukraine from NATO member states has presented Russian decisionmakers with a choice: allow Ukraine to receive arms and supplies from NATO or find a way to disrupt the flow of weapons making their way into Ukraine. Prior to the invasion, the choice for Russian leaders seemed clear to most Western analysts. "No one thought Russia would tolerate NATO assistance to Ukraine at this level prior to the war," according to one member of our expert panel. Russia's behavior since February 2022 has shown significant restraint, with only a few unsuccessful attempts to directly limit Western support for Ukraine. As mentioned earlier, Russia has attempted to coerce Western Europe by curtailing energy supplies. But there do not appear to have been any sustained Russian efforts to interdict NATO supply routes into Ukraine or to conduct strikes against supply depots or training facilities feeding Ukraine's military. There have been no shortage of general threats against NATO countries supporting Ukraine, but none have been linked to credible, specific escalatory actions. To this point, Russia's unwillingness to escalate horizontally to reduce military support to Ukraine has run counter to most observers' prewar expectations.

There are likely three explanations for Russian relative restraint to date, based on our brainstorming sessions. First, Russia appears to have a healthy fear of NATO's military capabilities and a strong desire to avoid a direct conflict with the Alliance, a conflict that it perceives might result from any direct attacks on NATO member states or personnel. These fears were compounded when Russian leaders' attempts to split NATO failed to achieve their goals and the Alliance showed an unanticipated level of cohesion and unity, in part as a reaction to Russian atrocities committed in Ukraine. Second, the failure of Russia's military efforts—particularly, battlefield losses and the depletion of critical weapons stockpiles, including precision munitions—has left Russian leaders with a more limited set of tools at their disposal should they choose to escalate against NATO and limited means of countering NATO retaliation following such a decision. Third, as discussed above, Russia may have at least initially believed that its more limited horizontal escalation efforts could work, allowing it to achieve its objective of curtailing NATO assistance to Ukraine without taking on further risks.

Ultimately, we do not know whether Russia's choice not to escalate horizontally further to this point in the war is a result of its fear of conflict with NATO in all conditions or tied to its misreading of NATO resolve and undue optimism regarding the likely effectiveness of other much more limited escalatory threats, such as those Russia has made to date. Had Russia been more successful early in the war, it may have been more willing to confront NATO; however, as its forces became bogged down and its forces depleted, the prospects of inviting another fight with NATO may have been too much risk for Russian leaders to accept. At the same time, as the ineffectiveness of Russian horizontal escalation measures to date becomes increasingly clear to the Kremlin, it may become willing to consider other, riskier options. At this point, our understanding of Russia's decisionmaking in the conflict is limited and should serve as a note of caution on assessments of Russia's willingness to escalate in the future if its situation continues to deteriorate. This issue will be discussed in greater detail in Chapter 3.

Overestimating the Effectiveness of Russian Escalatory Tools and Options

Russia does have, and has used, unconventional tools as an attempt to coerce its adversaries, both inside and outside Ukraine: information operations capabilities, control of energy supplies, and cyber operations tools. Many prewar assessments in the West overestimated the prospects of success for these tools of coercion. Attempts to starve and freeze populations through the withholding of energy resources or attacks on critical infrastructure ultimately failed to lead to a change in European or Ukrainian behavior, as did Russian attempts to win the information war within Western Europe. Ultimately, our brainstorming session pointed out that Russian leaders did not understand how international markets would adapt and that U.S. liquefied natural gas could help fill the gaps. Similarly, Ukraine's information operations tended to be far more effective than Russia's operations. Although the full extent of Russia's efforts to use cyber operations to escalate both in Ukraine and against NATO is beyond the scope of this report, the apparent lack of success in this arena suggests that these capabilities were less effective or less useful for escalation purposes than what prewar assessments posited. This appears to have left Russia pulling escalation levers that were less effective than feared.

Russia's Insular Decisionmaking

A key element that may have negatively affected Russia's use of economic coercion was the absence of Russian economic experts in the Kremlin's decisionmaking process. As Putin and his inner circle formulated escalatory or coercive responses to Western actions, they were often poorly equipped or ill-informed on key issues that should have influenced their decisionmaking. Likewise, decisions on military issues appear to have relied far less on military experts and quantitative assessments of military effectiveness than many Western analysts understood prior to the war. A good portion of Western assessments regarding Russian escalation decisionmaking and decision criteria was derived from studying Russia's General Staff and military science institutions. Many Western analysts, in turn, misunderstood the extent to which these materials and sources informed national-level decisions. In several cases, these sources provided distinct criteria designed to help military leaders assess military situations and suggested when decision points for escalation would be reached.

However, it is clear that Putin and his inner circle have not relied on this or other military advice, as evidenced by what one panel expert termed Russia's "shambolic plan for invasion." The lack of involvement of military expertise in Russian decisionmaking has left the Kremlin open to making large mistakes, and it has left Western analysts with the challenging task of trying to identify what information is reaching Putin and how likely he is to make escalation decisions largely separate from the advice of the broader Russian state.

In comparison with prewar assessments that frequently assumed a rigorous decisionmaking process based on expert inputs in such areas as military planning, economics, and foreign affairs, the war has revealed an insular, erratic decisionmaking process that may make future Kremlin escalation decisions unpredictable and prone to individual leaders' emotional and psychological states at any given time. Prior to the war, many Western analysts overestimated Russian willingness to escalate based on issues such as military assistance or Russian battlefield losses. Those criteria were, in part, tied to the West's understanding of Russian military planning constructs. However, the Kremlin's decisions to escalate or refrain from escalating, particularly against NATO, have highlighted a disconnect between highly quantitative and rational systems of military advice and the personalistic approach that Putin has relied on in past crises, including Russia's annexation of Crimea and its invasion of Eastern Ukraine in 2014.[3] A key feature of Putin's approach to decisionmaking since his return to power in 2012 has involved a narrowing of "the funnel of information that reached him to exclude the diplomats, economic ministers, and others who might have offered advice on the possible consequences of what was unfolding," which is manifested in his "making decisions alone and off the cuff."[4]

Putin's decisionmaking has also shown in past experiences, such as the sinking of the *Kursk* in 2000, the Dubrovka Theater siege in 2002, and Ukraine dating back to 2014 that major crises have affected him on a personal level, adding an element of emotion and anger to an already insular decisionmaking process that turned many policy decisions into highly personal affairs.[5] This emotional, irrational approach has involved a "habit of withdrawing," with Putin being "paralyzed into inaction" and unable to deal with fast-moving changes during crises.[6] For instance, during the Dubrovka Theater siege, Putin reportedly was "seized by panic at the events spiraling out of control in the world below."[7] In the future, this insularity

---

[3] Steven Lee Myers, *The New Tsar: The Rise and Reign of Vladimir Putin*, reprint ed., Knopf Doubleday Publishing Group, 2016, p. 461.

[4] Myers, 2016, pp. 461–462.

[5] Myers, 2016, pp. 474–475; Catherine Belton, *Putin's People: How the KGB Took Back Russia and Then Took on the West*, Farrar, Straus and Giroux, 2020, p. 241.

[6] Belton, 2020, p. 241.

[7] Belton, 2020, p. 243.

and the personal and emotional components of Putin's decisionmaking in major crises should reduce our confidence at both ends of the spectrum of escalation risks, both because personalized systems tend to be more prone to erratic changes in policy and approach and because Putin's prior management of crises displays a wide range of risk-taking and risk tolerance.[8]

Russia's Wartime Decisions on Escalation

The preceding sections highlight a series of misperceptions both in Russia and among Western countries that likely have shaped escalation choices to this point in the war. Although Western analysts tended to overestimate Russia's willingness to escalate prior to the invasion, in several cases, Russia has chosen escalatory courses of action. These actions mostly have taken place against Ukraine; but, in one major case, Russia did attempt nonmilitary escalation against Western European countries. In other cases, Russia has threatened escalatory responses, such as vague nuclear saber-rattling; however, Russia has ultimately refrained from acting.

Russian Escalation to Date

Russia's attempts to escalate have primarily been focused on Ukraine while largely avoiding actions against NATO members, including the United States.

Ukraine

Perhaps the two most significant examples of Russian escalation after the initial stages of the war involved attacks on civilian population centers and efforts to target critical infrastructure. In both cases, these acts were in response to Russian setbacks and most likely designed to both punish the Ukrainian population and break its will to fight. Russia may also have been

---

[8]   T. Clifton Morgan and Sally Howard Campbell, "Domestic Structure, Decisional Constraints, and War: So Why Kant Democracies Fight?" *Journal of Conflict Resolution*, Vol. 35, No. 2, June 1991; Anne Meng, "Accessing the State: Executive Constraints and Credible Commitment in Dictatorship," *Journal of Theoretical Politics*, Vol. 31, No. 4, 2019.

attempting to signal that Russia has a long-term advantage due to Russia's larger population and overall resources at its disposal and that Russia therefore remains capable of sustaining these attacks for as long as Ukraine intends to resist. As noted in earlier sections, the outcomes achieved by these attacks have been limited and likely have fallen well short of what Russian leaders sought. These attacks could also have been intended to send a signal to Russian elites and hard-liners regarding the Kremlin's resolve and determination to punish Ukrainian resistance in an effort to buttress internal support for the campaign.

NATO

The primary escalatory response aimed at European NATO members has been Russia's decision to cut energy supplies, with the hope that increased prices and scarce resources would compel European populations to turn against supporting Ukraine. Ultimately, this attempt at coercion did not work, in part because of European success in securing alternative energy supplies. Russia has also made repeated, somewhat opaque threats toward NATO on the risk of nuclear escalation in the conflict as a result of NATO support for Ukraine, a clear attempt at threatening escalation to coerce a change in behavior.[9] To date, these threats have largely been ignored by NATO members, or in any event have not been viewed as sufficiently credible to cause even serious debate about the merits of continuing assistance to Ukraine.

What has been most noteworthy to this point in the war has been the apparent absence of any efforts by Russia to conduct attacks against NATO support efforts in Ukraine. Although attempts to cut energy to European NATO members were widely predicted prior to the war, the apparent absence of a military response to NATO's support of Ukraine has been a surprise.

---

[9] Lauren Sukin, "Rattling the Nuclear Saber: What Russia's Nuclear Threats Really Mean," Carnegie Endowment for International Peace, May 4, 2023.

Why Russia Has Not Escalated More

Before considering future escalation pathways and risks, it is helpful to summarize the potential reasons why Russia has chosen not to escalate to a greater extent—primarily horizontally but also to a certain extent vertically—than it has to this point in the war. As discussed earlier in this chapter, our brainstorming sessions highlighted three main hypotheses that may help explain and, in doing so, provide a window into Russia's escalation decisions going forward. The first hypothesis our experts discussed was that NATO support to Ukraine has increased only gradually. One expert in our session used the "boiling frog" analogy to characterize both the incremental Western response to aiding Ukraine and Russia's muted response. Although this gradual effort might not have been intentional by NATO policymakers at the outset, the Alliance's support to Ukraine had been so incremental that Russian decisionmakers had time to adjust and were not faced with any major surprises. As a result, the situation gradually evolved and gave time for Russia's leaders to adapt to the new conditions, and no single change in assistance represented a dramatic enough change in Ukrainian capabilities to risk war with NATO to prevent it. Ultimately, because Russia's leaders were not caught off guard, their decisions could be more measured and less prone to emotional responses, and the gradual increases avoided creating a dramatic break point that might be seen in Moscow as forcing a decision between accepting defeat and risking escalation.

The second hypothesis is related to the first. It essentially contends that the information flow in the Russian system tends to filter out negative information while providing information that may be confirmatory or viewed favorably by Russian leaders, particularly Putin. This system may have created a view within the Kremlin that time is on Russia's side and, despite the military's setbacks, Russia's prospects for winning a protracted war are still high. As a result of this outlook, the Kremlin may not see a need to escalate further and risk conflict with NATO. Although somewhat comforting now (perhaps less so in the wake of the June 2023 Wagner mutiny), Russia's decisionmaking system and its filtering of information may leave Russian leaders more open to major shocks and surprises in the future if battlefield losses come suddenly or dramatically. This feature of the system may ultimately raise the risks of escalation to dangerous levels, particularly if Russian leaders are suddenly confronted with a threatening new reality that does not conform to their current favorable long-term outlook.

The third hypothesis, however, notes that Russia's acute concern for NATO military capabilities, particularly given the current weakened state of Russia's military, likely encourages Moscow to behave cautiously where it perceives that its actions could raise the risk of direct conflict with NATO. This would help to explain Russia's relative caution regarding military escalation horizontally in comparison with Russia's greater willingness to pursue and sustain high levels of intensity in its attacks on Ukraine. Russia's concern for NATO capabilities may not always serve to deter it from horizontal escalation, however. Should Russia come to believe that NATO direct intervention in the conflict is inevitable, for example, its insecurities regarding the damage NATO could inflict on it could also give Moscow an incentive to escalate first in an effort to either blunt the effectiveness of NATO strikes or to convince NATO not to undertake them. How all three of these hypotheses may affect Russian escalation decisions in the conflict going forward will be discussed in the subsequent chapter.

CHAPTER 3

Future Escalation in the War in Ukraine

Although the Russian invasion of Ukraine has produced extensive devastation and military losses, further escalation remains possible. Deliberate, inadvertent, and accidental escalation could all occur, though the circumstances and factors that would most plausibly contribute to each would likely vary. In this chapter, we will not spend substantial time analyzing purely accidental escalation scenarios, such as the crash of an aircraft due to weather or mechanical difficulties or the accidental firing of a weapon. We note that the potential for such accidents, and the risk that they might not be understood to be accidents by the opposing side, are likely to increase with the intensity of a conflict. However, apart from this observation, there is little that can be done to predict them.

Instead, we focus our attention on both inadvertent and deliberate escalation possibilities. The two are not fully distinct. A deliberate decision to escalate in one way may, for example, be perceived as a greater escalation than was intended, causing the opposite side to respond in an even more escalatory manner, a dynamic we discuss in greater detail below. But there are useful observations to be drawn from whether further escalation may begin either inadvertently or deliberately, so we discuss each possibility separately next.

The Risks of Inadvertent Escalation

The ongoing prosecution of the war by both Russia and, to a lesser extent, Ukraine carries with it risks for inadvertent escalation that have yet to materialize.[1] Certain NATO activities may carry similar risks. Observers of the conflict may become desensitized to these risks, as the war and these activities have been ongoing for some time without triggering notable horizontal escalation. But some of this success in avoiding horizontal escalation to date may be circumstantial and subject to change even absent any new intentional escalation decision on the part of any of the actors involved.

To better appreciate the current level of inadvertent escalatory risk involved in the conflict, we outline three plausible horizontal escalation scenarios based on what we know of Russian, Ukrainian, and NATO activities to date. This is by no means a comprehensive set of potential scenarios. But it helps to illustrate the types of risks of inadvertent escalation already present in the conflict to date, underlining the potential dangers of the protracted status quo.

Scenario 1: Russian Strikes Inside Ukraine Kill NATO Officials

Russia is engaged in a persistent air and missile campaign against numerous targets throughout Ukraine, including critical infrastructure, population centers, and military targets. Meanwhile, after having initially been heavily restricted in the early days of the war, officials from numerous NATO member states now visit Ukraine (particularly Kyiv) on a regular basis. A Russian missile barrage that takes place during such a visit could quite plausibly kill the visiting NATO officials, joining the thousands of Ukrainians who have died in similar attacks. Although Russia may not have intended to target the NATO officials specifically, such an explanation may not be

---

[1] The risks of inadvertent escalation from Ukrainian actions are likely more limited due to the comparatively limited nature of Ukrainian military capabilities. Although Russia and NATO have substantial military capabilities that they have not yet employed in the conflict, including nuclear capabilities, Ukraine does not. Russian and NATO actions, therefore, have the potential to create circumstances in which the other may perceive a need to strike preemptively or act specifically to deter further attacks. Because Ukraine has no similar set of capabilities held in reserve, its actions in general are likely to have less inadvertent escalatory risk. One notable exception to this could be dramatic Ukrainian battlefield success that threatens the Russian military position in Ukraine and that could be the precursor to different potential Russian intentional escalation decisions.

believed by the NATO member state. Depending on the state and the officials involved, this could lead to political pressure for a unilateral attack on a Russian target or to diplomatic demands for a collective NATO response. Russia, in turn, could decide either to wait and see on a possible NATO response or attempt to preempt any such attack by striking relevant NATO capabilities first. Either possibility could lead to a direct exchange of fire between Russian and NATO militaries, a situation that both sides have been working assiduously to avoid since February 2022.

Scenario 2: Aggressive Russian Maneuvers Against U.S. Surveillance Aircraft Kill U.S. Military Personnel

Russia has established a pattern of aggressive, risky behavior toward U.S. military assets, both during and preceding the war in Ukraine across many locations throughout Europe.[2] Although such behavior has not yet led to the deaths of any U.S. service members, Russia appears quite willing to run the risk that it might. Aggressive Russian maneuvers similar to those that led to the crash of the unmanned MQ-9 aircraft in March 2023 that instead targeted a manned U.S. surveillance aircraft operating in or near the Black Sea, such as an E-P3 or P-8, could quite plausibly lead to the deaths of at least some of the U.S. personnel on board. Furthermore, the United States may have limited understanding of the extent to which the Russian actions that led to the crash were intentional or inadvertent.

Such an event would present U.S. policymakers with a difficult decision. U.S. policy on the war in Ukraine has prioritized avoiding direct military involvement in the conflict. At the same time, U.S. leaders are unlikely to establish any precedent that Russia, or any other country, can engage in reckless behavior leading to the deaths of U.S. service members without repercussions. Therefore, it is plausible that the United States would consider a direct military response to the incident, possibly by targeting the Russian aircraft or supporting base involved. If Russia believes its own role

---

2   Nahal Toosi and Lawrence Ukenye, "Russian Jet's Collision with U.S. Drone Sparks Diplomatic Flurry," *Politico*, March 14, 2023; Elizabeth McLaughlin and Luis Martinez, "A Look at the US Military's Close Calls with Russia in the Air and at Sea," *ABC News*, April 9, 2020.

in the incident to be accidental, it may view any U.S. strike as a highly escalatory measure and possibly indicative of a U.S. reconsideration of its policy of avoiding direct involvement in Ukraine. This may, in turn, lead Russia to consider further retaliatory strikes of its own, establishing a pattern of direct military confrontation between the two nuclear powers.

Scenario 3: Russia Misperceives NATO Moves as Signal of Inevitable Intervention in Ukraine

Russia's invasion of Ukraine has substantially increased the concerns of eastern flank NATO members for their own security. These concerns have led to steps to increase NATO military capabilities in and around these countries, although to date these increases have remained comparatively modest.[3] Although Russia has been (and likely remains) highly concerned over the presence of NATO long-range strike capabilities near its borders, the Alliance has not included such capabilities in the posture enhancements that have been undertaken in eastern member states since February 2022.

However, risks of Russian misperceptions of NATO intentions remain, and they may not be confined to the military domain. For example, a robust increase in higher-readiness forces with longer-range strike capabilities that was accompanied by explicit political discussions about a pathway to membership for Ukraine in NATO, or other comparable security guarantees, could convince Moscow that it has entered a slippery slope to inevitable direct NATO intervention into the war in Ukraine. Faced with such a conclusion, Russia may decide to push for a ceasefire and terminate the conflict, but it could also plausibly decide to strike NATO targets preemptively to either degrade NATO intervention capabilities or deter such a future intervention by underlining its own willingness to bring the war directly to NATO countries. In response to what it would likely view as an unprovoked Russian attack, NATO could, in turn, be deterred, fearing further escalation, but it could also be outraged and seek to punish Moscow through direct military action against Russia. Moscow, in turn, would face difficult

---

[3] North Atlantic Treaty Organization, "NATO's Military Presence in the East of the Alliance," webpage, updated December 21, 2022.

decisions regarding whether to then respond in kind or seek an off-ramp. But the risks of a spiral of further escalation would be clear.

Implications of Inadvertent Escalation Risks

All three of these scenarios describe the beginnings of potential spirals of horizontal escalation that could end in dramatically higher-intensity forms of conflict than those with which they began, including potentially nuclear use. It may seem difficult to imagine that a conflict that ends in nuclear exchange could begin with an inadvertent strike or diplomatic signal, and certainly most such events do not escalate in this manner. But if such initial exchanges expand to threaten the core interests or regime survival of one or both of the parties, then escalation to much higher levels of conflict becomes plausible. Russia's acute insecurity regarding U.S. and NATO military capabilities and intentions has long been thought to create conditions where direct conflict between Russia and NATO could quickly escalate to the point where Russia would become concerned for its own survival.[4] At that point, Russia may seek off-ramps to the conflict, and NATO would be wise to be attuned to such signals, but it may instead seek to demonstrate its resolve and deter feared NATO nuclear attacks by being the first to cross the nuclear threshold. Such risks, to a greater or lesser degree, hang over any instance of direct conflict between nuclear-armed states.

U.S. policymakers appear to be acutely aware of these risks and, to date, have been assiduous in avoiding several circumstances that could bring about direct NATO-Russia conflict, including by explicitly and publicly ruling out direct U.S. intervention in the Ukraine war, by (1) altering U.S. surveillance activities to reduce the risks of contact with Russian forces and (2) limiting the scale and types of military assets deployed to Europe during the conflict.[5] What the scenarios above illustrate, however, is that such efforts are not foolproof. Given the stakes of the conflict for Russia, some

---

[4]   Bryan Frederick, Matthew Povlock, Stephen Watts, Miranda Priebe, and Edward Geist, *Assessing Russian Reactions to U.S. and NATO Posture Enhancements*, RAND Corporation, RR-1879-AF, 2017.

[5]   Nahal Toosi, "The Line Biden Won't Cross on Ukraine," *Politico*, February 23, 2022; Jim Sciutto, "New US Drone Routes Over Black Sea 'Definitely Limit' Intelligence Gathering, Says US Official," CNN, March 28, 2023.

potential for inadvertent escalation is likely to persist for the duration of the conflict, highlighting the value of maintaining open lines of military and diplomatic communications with Russia to help reduce the risk that such spirals as these cannot be stopped should they get underway.

The Risks of Deliberate Escalation

Notwithstanding concerns about inadvertent escalation, the possibility that Russia may decide to escalate its involvement deliberately or intentionally in the ongoing war in Ukraine remains perhaps the central concern for U.S. and allied policymakers. Despite the horrific toll the war has already exacted on Ukrainian civilians, from a military perspective Russia retains several options to escalate the conflict. Russia's failure to achieve its key objectives in Ukraine, or even to maintain the territorial position it achieved in the early days of the invasion, at its current level of escalation provides Russia with a clear motivation to consider (and to have considered) more escalatory approaches to the war. Absent an unexpected shift in battlefield conditions that dramatically favors Russia at the current level of escalation, U.S. and allied policymakers would be prudent to carefully assess the conditions under which further Russian escalation might occur and the forms it may take.

The possibility that Ukraine or NATO may decide to escalate their involvement in the conflict is also important to consider. Although Ukrainian capabilities are much more limited than Russian capabilities, providing them with fewer escalatory options, certain options remain available to Kyiv, most notably a more concerted campaign of strikes inside Russia. NATO member states, by contrast, have enormous potential capabilities to call on should they decide to become directly involved in the conflict, but much more limited motivation to do so. The potential for Ukrainian or NATO deliberate escalation will be discussed in greater detail at the end of this chapter.

Overall, though, this section focuses on possible types of future deliberate Russian escalation in the ongoing war in Ukraine as the actor with the greatest capability and motivation to pursue further escalation. Although this discussion focuses on intentional Russian decisions to escalate and identifies conditions that may make such decisions more likely, the potential for inadvertent escalation pressures to come into play following a deliberate decision are also discussed.

Russian Assessment of the Current Situation

Russia faces several challenges in the ongoing conflict as of summer 2023. The Russian campaign against Ukrainian critical infrastructure throughout the previous fall and winter does not appear to have degraded Ukrainian commitment to the war, and neither has the reduction in Russian gas and oil provided to Europe fractured NATO and European Union (EU) consensus in favor of continuing support to Ukraine. In contrast with historical examples of foreign invasions of Russia itself, Moscow was not able to rely on winter temperatures to substantially shift the diplomatic or military battlefield in its favor. Furthermore, Russia's partial mobilization campaign, underway since September 2022, appears to have at most stabilized the front lines but not to have given Russia any new or decisive advantage. The June 2023 Wagner mutiny also highlighted the extent to which the demands of sustaining the invasion of Ukraine have affected the Kremlin's ability to ensure domestic stability.

Complicating assessments of Russian behavior is the uncertainty around precisely what Russian goals are at this point in the conflict. Russia's initial aims in the February 2022 invasion appear to have focused on changing the regime in Kyiv and ensuring that Ukraine's westward shift was halted and its orientation was durably shifted away from Europe and toward Moscow.[6] The failure of the initial attempt to seize Kyiv and the strength of subsequent Ukrainian national resistance appear to have put those goals out of reach. Moscow then appears to have shifted to a more prosaic goal of territorial conquest, as confirmed by the illegal annexation of four Ukrainian provinces in October 2022.[7] As of this writing, roughly one-quarter of the Ukrainian

---

[6] Zack Beauchamp, "Why Is Putin Attacking Ukraine? He Told Us," Vox, February 23, 2022; Ian Hill, "Russia's Invasion of Ukraine: Why and Why Now?" *The Interpreter*, June 22, 2023.

[7] Adam Schreck, "Putin Signs Annexation of Ukrainian Regions as Losses Mount," Associated Press, October 5, 2022.

territory that Russia has formally claimed remains outside Russian control.[8] Conquering this territory is one of Russia's likely war aims, as is preventing Ukraine from retaking the territory Russia previously seized, including Crimea. Avoiding a Russian domestic perception, both popularly and among the elite, that the Kremlin lost the war is also likely an important war aim, given the risks that leaders who lose conflicts face of being removed from power.[9] But whether Russia retains additional goals that it might be willing to consider further escalation to achieve regarding the orientation of Ukraine's foreign policy or security arrangements is less clear.

As of this writing, Russia appears to still be planning for a war of attrition intended to eventually fracture either Ukrainian capabilities and will or Western support for Kyiv, allowing it to achieve its territorial aims but with diminishing near-term prospects for either event. However, the Wagner mutiny highlights the risks of such a strategy in ways that are likely clear even to a Kremlin that has been receiving biased or incomplete information about the state of the conflict. The commitment of resources to the invasion of Ukraine has left the Kremlin's control of Russia itself brittle, increasing domestic perceptions of Kremlin weakness.[10] Although Wagner does not appear to have intended to threaten the regime itself, its apparent ability to do so cannot have been lost on other figures and actors inside Russia, including the regime itself.[11] The risks for the regime that such fragility underscores may reduce the Kremlin's appetite for a protracted war of attrition and encourage the consideration of options that might shorten the

[8] Pablo Gutiérrez and Ashley Kirk, "A Year of War: How Russian Forces Have Been Pushed Back in Ukraine," *The Guardian*, February 21, 2023; George Barros, Kateryna Stepanenko, Thomas Bergeron, Noel Mikkelsen, and Daniel Mealie, "Interactive Map: Russia's Invasion of Ukraine," Institute for the Study of War and American Enterprise Institute's Critical Threats Project, undated.

[9] George W. Downs and David M. Rocke, "Conflict, Agency, and Gambling for Resurrection: The Principal-Agent Problem Goes to War," *American Journal of Political Science*, Vol. 38, No. 2, May 1994.

[10] Anthony Faiola, Fredrick Kunkle, Robyn Dixon, and Catherine Belton, "Putin Rules by Showing Strength. Russia's Crisis Exposed His Weakness," *Washington Post*, June 25, 2023.

[11] "Russian Mercenary Chief Says He Did Not Intend Coup, Putin Thanks Those Who Stood Down," Reuters, June 26, 2023.

war. Withdrawal from Ukraine is one such option, but one that would bring its own set of risks for regime stability given the likely reaction of domestic far-right nationalist figures.[12] Attempting to shorten the war by pursuing greater escalation is another.

Therefore, the general incentives for further Russian escalation seem clear: to attempt to decisively shift the conflict in Moscow's favor, allowing Russia to defeat Ukraine militarily and avert future losses and other costs that seem set to accumulate indefinitely, further weakening the regime. However, as discussed above, some of these incentives to escalate have been in place for Moscow for some time, at least since the failure of the initial effort to take Kyiv in the opening days of the war. Russia has bowed to escalatory pressures at least twice, in the September 2022 decision to undertake partial mobilization and in the subsequent October 2022 decision to extensively target Ukrainian critical infrastructure through missile strikes.

Could Russia decide to escalate still further in the future? Our discussions and assessments identified more steps that Russia could potentially take in the war in Ukraine but appears to have been restrained from doing so to date. We identify six options for intentional escalation that Russia could pursue in its war in Ukraine. These options are certainly not exhaustive, and other—or similar—variations are possible. In selecting these options for assessment, we focused on escalation options with the potential to alter the dynamics of the conflict most fundamentally. Russia may decide to mobilize its population and economy more fully on a war footing to enhance its ability to produce and sustain military capabilities as an example of escalatory options that we did not include as a result. This step would reflect a decision to escalate the conflict, as did the September 2022 partial mobilization discussed above. But the effects on the dynamics of the conflict at this stage would likely be easier to anticipate and more gradual. In the following options we assess, we focus on escalatory options that risk introducing novel or particularly dangerous dynamics to the conflict because these options are likely the most important for assessments in informing policymaker decisions and public debate.

---

[12] Alexey Kovalev, "Putin Has a New Opposition—and It's Furious at Defeat in Ukraine," *Foreign Policy*, September 12, 2022.

Under each option, we briefly identify the likely *motivations* that could prompt Russia to take this step, a brief assessment of whether Russia likely retains the *capabilities* to take this step as of summer 2023, and finally the *restraining factors* that may have inhibited Moscow from taking this step to this point. These restraining factors may therefore also serve as potential indicators or warnings of factors that, should they begin to erode or diminish over the course of the war, could indicate an increased likelihood of this type of intentional Russian escalation. We organize these options below into categories depending on whether they primarily involve *horizontal escalation*, or escalation outside the geographic boundaries of Ukraine; *vertical escalation*, involving a clear escalation in the intensity or nature of Russian attacks inside Ukraine; or escalation options involving nuclear weapons that would have important horizontal and vertical escalation dimensions.

Russian Horizontal Escalation Options

We identified two main potential intentional horizontal escalation options for Russia in the ongoing war: a limited Russian attack against a NATO target in Europe or a collaboration with a Russian partner to provoke a crisis outside Europe that might split U.S. or NATO attention.[13] We considered the possibility of a large-scale Russian attack on NATO as well but do not cover it in detail below for two reasons. First, we could not identify a plausible Russian motivation to intentionally start a large-scale war with NATO under circumstances in which its own military capabilities have already been so substantially degraded and in which Russia therefore likely assesses that it would lose. The fear of such a conflict is likely an important factor in restraining Russian escalation to date (as will be discussed in greater detail later in this chapter). Although a limited Russian attack on NATO could plausibly be undertaken to attempt to coerce changes in NATO behavior—such as levels of support for Ukraine—by threatening further, likely nuclear,

---

[13] We also considered potential Russian escalation attempts in the cyber or space domains. However, identifying plausible scenarios for when Russia might do more, and why, is challenging because of the lack of clarity in open sources regarding what Russia may or may not have done in these domains. Therefore, we focused on scenarios for which the relevant history of prior Russian actions could be fully discussed and appreciated.

escalation, a large-scale Russian attack on NATO would be relatively more likely to precipitate a highly damaging NATO counterattack. Second, however, we note that a large-scale Russian attack on NATO may be plausible through inadvertent escalation pathways, such as those that may begin with a Russian misperception of the risk that NATO intends a large-scale attack on Russia. Although this risk is certainly important for policymakers to consider, this report focuses on Russian deliberate escalation decisions, so we exclude such a scenario below.

Limited Russian Attack Against NATO in Europe

This option would involve Russia undertaking a limited strike or set of strikes against NATO targets in Europe, most likely on the territory of a European NATO member state.[14] Such an attack could vary widely in scale or intensity, from a single strike at a target designed to produce no casualties to a more sustained barrage against a set of militarily or politically significant targets that would cause substantial casualties.[15] Although the specifics of the Russian attack would greatly affect how the United States and NATO might choose to respond, any Russian decision to undertake such an attack would have certain common characteristics, including in the motivation to undertake the attack and the factors that may currently be restraining Russia from attempting it.

Motivation

The primary motivation of a limited Russian attack against NATO would likely be to attempt to coerce NATO member states to limit or cease the

---

[14] Russia may have attacked a NATO target operating over international waters in the March 14, 2023, downing of an MQ-9 unmanned aircraft system (UAS), although whether the contact with the UAS was intentional or inadvertent remains unclear. Either way, though, the fact that the intentionality of the attack was unclear and the fact that it did not take place on the territory of a NATO member state limit any potential signals Russia may or may not have intended to send regarding the escalatory risks of continued support to Ukraine (see Eric Schmitt, "Russian Warplane Hits American Drone over Black Sea, U.S. Says," *New York Times*, March 14, 2023).

[15] For an example of the types of limited attack scenarios that Russia could contemplate, see Bryan Frederick, Samuel Charap, and Karl P. Mueller, *Responding to a Limited Russian Attack on NATO During the Ukraine War*, RAND Corporation, PE-A2081-1, December 2022.

support they are providing to Ukraine.[16] By demonstrating a willingness to attack NATO directly, Russia could signal a willingness to escalate still further and impose additional costs on NATO member countries if support for Kyiv was not restricted. Alternately, Russia could undertake such an attack to coerce NATO into restraining Ukraine more directly, such as by pressuring Kyiv not to undertake further offensive operations against Russian forces in Ukrainian territory. Either motivation would follow a similar logic: threaten to impose greater costs directly on NATO member states as a means of limiting Ukrainian capabilities or operations in ways that Russia has proven unable to do using military force inside Ukraine.

Capability to Execute

Russia's capability to execute such an attack would likely vary widely depending on the scale and nature of the attack under consideration. Russia certainly retains sufficient long-range strike capabilities to attack an individual or small number of targets inside NATO, particularly if they are undefended. Larger-scale strikes on NATO could be hampered by the demands of operations in Ukraine and by the expenditure of munitions and loss of capabilities in the conflict.

However, shortcomings in Russia's long-range strikes on Ukrainian targets over the past several months, including in targeting, accuracy, and ability to evade Ukrainian air defenses could limit Russia's confidence in being able to execute a strike against its intended target. Moreover, the degradation in Russian military capabilities during the war also likely reduces the conventional military threat that NATO members would perceive Moscow to be making, reducing their likelihood of being coerced by the threat. Russia's capability to execute nuclear strikes, however, likely remains intact.

It is also worth noting that using an overt military strike to coerce a change in NATO behavior likely would not be Russia's first choice. In the past, Russia appears to have sent similar coercive signals through more-

---

[16] Russia could also attempt to directly attack supply lines and interdict key capabilities directly, but given the scale of assistance being provided to Ukraine, such an approach would likely have much greater military requirements that may be beyond Russia's current capabilities.

covert means.[17] It is possible that such a covert attack may still be the first option that Russia tries in the future to attempt to coerce NATO more directly. But as the war drags on, and as large numbers of Russian personnel are expelled from NATO countries, it is also possible that Russia's ability to execute a more covert option may be degraded, leaving it with more overt, conventional military options.

Restraining Factors

If Russia has a clear motivation to undertake such an attack, and likely retains the capabilities to undertake at least a smaller-scale version of such an attack, the question then becomes, why has it not done so? We identify at least six factors that have likely served to restrain Russia from undertaking such an attack and that may or may not continue to do so in the future:

1. **Russia believes it still has a path to achieving its goals in Ukraine.** At present, there still appears to be a perception in the Kremlin that continued mobilization and the potential to outproduce Ukraine and key NATO countries in critical munitions may enable Russia to win a long, grinding war of attrition, without taking on further risks of NATO intervention. Directly attacking NATO and hoping that the response would be a reduction in support for Ukraine rather than an increase, or even direct NATO entry into the war, would be an enormous risk for Russia to run. As long as Moscow believes it has other, plausible pathways to achieving its goals in the war, it may prefer to avoid such risks.

2. **Russia does not see direct NATO intervention as inevitable.** The United States and other key NATO member states have been clear since before the outset of the war that they do not intend to intervene directly in Ukraine. Should Russia come to believe that direction NATO intervention is inevitable, even if not necessarily imminent, it could greatly reduce the risks that Russian policymakers feel they

---

[17] Andrew Higgins and Hana de Goeij, "Czechs Blame 2014 Blasts at Ammunition Depots on Elite Russian Spy Unit," *New York Times*, April 17, 2021; Andrius Sytas, "Estonia Says It Repelled Major Cyber Attack After Removing Soviet Monuments," Reuters, August 18, 2022.

may be running by attacking NATO directly first and may even provide a motivation to do so proactively.

3. **Russian perceptions of NATO cohesion and resolve in response to an attack.** Critical to the Russian perception that an attack on NATO would be a high-risk gambit are the assumptions inside the Kremlin about how NATO would likely respond. Russia likely assesses that NATO has the military capacity to respond in a devastating fashion, should it choose to do so. The question of whether Russia perceives NATO as likely to be unified and aggressive in its reaction to a Russian attack, or whether it perceives that NATO would become divided and afraid of further escalation, is therefore likely to be a critical factor in informing Russian assessments of the advisability of such an attack. To date, NATO decisionmaking in the war has been, on the whole, highly cohesive, and there has been clear, widespread public and elite support for Ukraine, which Russia may assess makes it more challenging to coerce a change in this support. Should these conditions change, such as through a change in government in key NATO member states (particularly, the United States), then Russian perceptions of the likelihood that a coercive attack on NATO could succeed may shift as well.

4. **Restrictions on NATO-provided support to Ukraine.** The United States and other key NATO members appear to have placed restrictions on the employment of the military capabilities they have provided to Ukraine. In particular, these assets appear to have been provided under the condition that they are not used to undertake strikes inside Russian territory. Given the dependence of Kyiv on NATO for assistance in the war, these conditions likely do at least in part constrain Ukraine's use of these weapons. They also represent another area of risk for Russia where NATO could—potentially very quickly—shift its policy in response to a Russian attack on NATO, increasing the costs and risks that Russia may run as a result. Should this NATO policy shift or loosen beforehand, however, it could reduce Russian incentives to avoid such an attack.

5. **Gradual increases in NATO assistance.** NATO's assistance to Ukraine has increased substantially over the course of the war, both in scale and in the sophistication of the systems being provided. It

has also increased very gradually, however. There has been no single decision or point in time that represented a critical moment for Russia to attempt to coerce an end to NATO support to Ukraine. Instead, each increase has been only slightly greater than what came before and has often been accompanied by uncertainty regarding timelines or scale. As a result, Russia has had less motivation to undertake a high-risk strategy to prevent any particular increase in support for Kyiv. A future increase that departed from this pattern and was viewed in Moscow as fundamentally changing the trajectory of the conflict, such as by making Ukrainian victory inevitable, might create stronger incentives for Russia to run greater risks to avoid it.

6. **No acute threats to Russian domestic stability.** As discussed above, domestic instability has the potential to create pressures for Russian escalation. To date, despite the Wagner mutiny, such instability appears to be limited. Russia has not experienced widespread domestic unrest sufficient to threaten the stability of the regime, despite the effects of international sanctions, conscription, and other hardships borne by the Russian people as a result of the war, or despite the poor performance of the Russian military to date and resulting dissatisfaction from nationalist figures. The Kremlin has invested heavily for years to help ensure domestic stability, including through the state domination of the media environment and investment in domestic security services. As long as the regime remains confident in this stability, this reduces a possible incentive for the Kremlin to take larger risks to end the war more quickly on its terms. That is, relative Russian domestic stability is an important condition for Moscow to continue to believe that its military strategy still has time to succeed with the current regime in power and that it need not take on further escalation risks at this time. Should Moscow come to believe that regime stability may be under threat, it may be willing to run larger risks to avoid prolonging a war that may threaten the survival of the regime.

Provoke Out-of-Area Crisis

Russia could also attempt to incentivize one of its partners in a different region to create a crisis outside Europe that would demand U.S. or allied attention, but in which Russia may not be directly involved. Such a crisis could take a variety of forms, from a crisis involving the Iranian nuclear program, to North Korea threats, to neighboring U.S. allies in the Indo-Pacific, to one involving a Venezuelan threat to regional stability. To be effective, however, the crisis would need to threaten sufficiently important U.S. interests to prompt the shift of substantial U.S. policymaker attention and military resources. That is, it would likely not be limited to a purely diplomatic or political set of actions or statements on the part of the Russian partner.

Motivation

The Russian motivation for provoking such a crisis would be to shift U.S. and allied attention elsewhere to reduce the scale and cohesiveness of support for Ukraine. Most directly, U.S. or allied military capabilities deployed elsewhere would then not be available to be provided to Ukraine. Indirectly, clear demonstrations and reminders of the global scope of U.S. security commitments could give U.S. policymakers pause in continuing to provide munitions stocks, scarce systems such as Patriot batteries, and other resources to Ukraine, at least at current levels. Incentivizing a Russian partner to provoke the crisis rather than doing so itself in a different region could also have the advantage for Russia of dividing Western political and diplomatic focus on the punishment of Russia for its invasion of Ukraine.

Capability to Execute

Incentivizing another state to provoke a crisis in this manner would likely be quite challenging for Moscow, unless the state was already predisposed to do so for its own reasons. The state would face substantial potential risks and costs from provoking a crisis sufficiently acute to alter U.S. and allied strategic calculations, exposing itself to potential threats or sanctions to essentially do a favor for the Kremlin. Russia has a range of financial and military relationships with its partners and could promise future benefits in the form of military technology and support or direct financial considerations. However, Russia's struggles in the current conflict limit the resources it has available and would also likely make it more difficult for Moscow to credibly promise that it would be in a position to provide future benefits, shifting any negotiation over the potential terms of such an agreement in favor of the partner and increasing the costs for the Kremlin. More promising for Russia is the possibility that a partner might be interested in provoking a crisis for its own reasons, whether related to its domestic political challenges or its own strategic calculations, to which Russia could provide more limited forms of encouragement or support.

Restraining Factors

There are at least two key factors that are likely restraining Russia from pursuing horizontal escalation in this manner, beyond the limited ability of Russia to incentivize partners to take these steps, as discussed earlier:

1. **Russian unwillingness to take further risks.** An international crisis of sufficient severity to shift U.S. or allied strategic calculations would likely bring with it substantial escalation risks of its own. Although these would likely be borne first by the Russian partner involved, there would remain the possibility that Russia could be drawn into any resulting conflict—for example, if the Russian partner were to be on the verge of collapse (a condition that precipitated Russian intervention in the Syrian civil war)—or that other states could be drawn into Russia's conflict with Ukraine out of a desire to retaliate against Russia for its role in any potential conflict, particularly if Russian involvement in starting the crisis became known. Although these risks might vary substantially depending on the nature of the crisis, in general terms these would represent additional risks for Russia to balance against the potential benefits of distracting U.S. or allied focus on Ukraine.

2. **Potential for hardening of international opposition to Russia.** Although Russia's aggression in Ukraine has been strongly condemned and opposed by most Western democratic states, the reaction toward Russia in much of the rest of the world has been more ambivalent, with, for example, very few states that are not U.S. allies joining the multilateral sanctions imposed on Russia. Russian instigation of an additional crisis elsewhere in the world, should its involvement become known, would risk widening perceptions that Russia is a broader threat to international peace and security, in turn

widening the coalition of states willing to take active diplomatic and economic steps to oppose its aggression.

Russian Vertical Escalation Options

Although Russia has escalated its war against Ukraine substantially, including widespread attacks on civilian targets and massive applications of Russian military resources, there are likely still additional options available to Russia to escalate the conflict inside Ukraine. Next, we discuss two: (1) an intensified Russian air and missile campaign to establish air superiority over Ukraine and (2) the large-scale usage of chemical weapons against either military or civilian targets.[18] These two represent the most plausible remaining escalation options inside Ukraine that we could identify that would clearly differ from the present Russian approach. Nuclear escalation also remains quite plausible in this conflict, but we discuss those possibilities in a separate section in this chapter because nuclear use would inherently involve both vertical and horizontal dimensions.

Sustained Russian Air and Missile Campaign

In contrast with its heavily depleted ground forces, Russian Aerospace Forces (VKS) have survived the first year and a half of the war in Ukraine comparatively intact.[19] Russia appears to have been hesitant to make fuller use of these forces for a variety of reasons, discussed in the following sections, but their condition provides Russia with at least the theoretical option to escalate their use and make airpower a greater part of the Russian campaign against Ukraine.

---

[18] We also considered the possibility of Russian biological weapons use. While possible, biological weapons would likely be much more difficult to control and use for battlefield purposes, although they could plausibly be used as a weapon of terror against civilian populations. For these reasons, we considered their use by Russia in Ukraine to be less plausible than the other options highlighted here.

[19] Chris Gordon, "Russian Air Force 'Has Lot of Capability Left' One Year on from Ukraine Invasion," *Air and Space Forces Magazine*, February 15, 2023.

Motivation

The main advantage Russia could in principle gain from such an initiative would likely be to establish some measure of air superiority in the skies over Ukraine. Currently, Russian progress in its ground campaign is likely being hindered by the inability of the VKS to provide effective support to Russian advances, to reliably attack and destroy Ukrainian targets, or to prevent limited Ukrainian air operations. If it could be established, Russian control of the skies could be an important factor helping to shift the conflict in Moscow's favor. Despite these potential benefits, a fulsome effort to use the VKS toward this end does not appear to have been attempted.

Capability to Execute

It is entirely possible that Russia has not attempted such a sustained air campaign because it does not assess the capability of the VKS in achieving such a goal. We know little about Russian assessments of the state of its air forces from open sources, including Russian perceptions of the effectiveness of the VKS to date in missions. But the continued operation and resilience of Ukrainian air defense assets so long into the war, despite tremendous numbers of Russian missiles fired in the conflict at both military and civilian targets, suggest that Russia may face serious challenges in targeting and destroying Ukrainian air defenses. A concerted application of the VKS to this problem could bring successes, but it could also come at the cost of serious losses in aircraft and trained pilots that may be more difficult for Russia to replace than it would be for Ukraine to field replacement air defense systems. Given the assistance provided by the United States and key NATO allies (e.g., Patriot batteries), it is possible that Ukrainian air defenses may be in a better position relative to the VKS than they were at the outset of the conflict, although this is difficult to assess with any certainty.

Restraining Factors

Beyond the possibility that Russia may simply be unable to succeed at establishing air superiority in Ukraine, there are likely several factors that are restraining Russia from attempting this option.

1. **Russian desire to preserve capabilities for NATO:** Notwithstanding the military challenges it faces in Ukraine, Russia retains substantial concern for the need—in its view—to continue to deter

potential NATO aggression against Russia. Russia views any NATO attack as likely to heavily involve NATO aerospace assets, stemming from observations of past U.S. campaigns from Iraq to the Balkans. Therefore, Russia likely believes that maintaining its own aerospace forces in relatively good condition may be an important part of deterring a NATO attack, which it continues to fear.

2. **Difficulty of replacing lost aircraft and pilots:** Under any conditions, the need to replace an expensive aircraft that was shot down by a less expensive air defense missile can create an unfavorable exchange ratio. This factor was the logic behind Russia's substantial investment in air defense assets designed to counter NATO air capabilities. Russia's present circumstances would make such an exchange exceedingly challenging given the high costs of the war to date for Russia and the effects of international sanctions that may make acquiring needed components for sophisticated aircraft more difficult. Unlike other military assets (e.g., UASs, artillery shells, or small arms that can likely be acquired from other countries), Russia likely has few if any options for purchasing replacement aircraft from abroad, given the small number of countries that produce advanced military aircraft, the fact that most of those that do are U.S. allies, and that others, including the People's Republic of China (PRC), may remain hesitant to share their own advanced military technology with Moscow. Repurchases of Russian or even Soviet manufactured planes previously sold to other countries could remain a viable alternative for acquiring less advanced aircraft, however. Similar concerns likely apply to the replacement of Russian pilots who would be lost in a more concerted air campaign. Although Russia has proven willing to replace infantry losses with conscripts with minimal training, it may not feel similarly confident in its ability to quickly replace more experienced pilots.

3. **Public and diplomatic reaction to high-profile losses:** Even if ultimately successful, a concerted Russian air campaign would likely lead to large numbers of highly visible losses, especially in the initial phases. Videos of many Russian aircraft being destroyed in flight would likely enhance both domestic and international uncertainty

regarding Russia's military competence in the campaign, potentially undercutting support for the Kremlin's efforts.

4. **Russia believes it still has a path to achieving its goals in Ukraine:** Similar to the factor noted above that likely restrains Russia from directly attacking NATO, Moscow likely still believes it has a pathway to achieving its goals in Ukraine absent further escalation, through prevailing in essentially a war of attrition. This perception may or may not be based on accurate information, but as long as it persists, it is likely to restrain Russia from taking on further, high-cost risks.

5. **No acute threats to Russian domestic stability:** As also noted above, if the Kremlin believes that its control of Russia remains stable, it is more likely to believe that it has time to wait for its current approach to the war to succeed, and it does not need to run undue risks to achieve its goals in Ukraine more quickly. Should Moscow come to believe that regime stability may be under threat, it may be willing to run larger risks to avoid prolonging a war that may threaten the survival of the regime.

Larger-Scale Russian Chemical Weapons Use

To date, Russia has been credibly accused of limited use of chemical agents in Ukraine, including phosphorous.[20] However, Russia could decide to (1) substantially expand its use of chemical agents and (2) escalate the types of agents used—from phosphorous to deadlier nerve gasses, such as Novichok.[21] It could use these agents on the battlefield against Ukrainian forces, either to blunt a Ukrainian advance or to support a Russian attack, or against primarily civilian targets.

Motivation

Russia could have two different motivations for the large-scale use of chemical weapons in Ukraine. First, Russia could potentially see battlefield advan-

---

[20] Matt Murphy, "Ukraine War: Russia Accused of Using Phosphorous Bombs in Bakhmut," BBC News, May 6, 2023.

[21] Joby Warrick, "A Legacy of 'Secrecy and Deception': Why Russia Clings to an Outlawed Chemical Arsenal," *Washington Post*, March 19, 2022.

tages to the employment of these weapons. Although chemical weapons have historically proven difficult to employ effectively, as will be discussed in the following sections, there may be specific circumstances involving massed Ukrainian forces that are not prepared for chemical weapons use that Russia could assess to be advantageous. Second, Russia could see the widespread use of chemical weapons as an opportunity to wear down or break Ukrainian civilian and military morale or to shock NATO members into pushing Ukraine to the negotiating table for fear of further escalation.

Capability to Execute

Although Russia was supposed to have destroyed its arsenal of chemical weapons in 2017, there is substantial evidence that it has not done so.[22] However, the size and scope of Russia's chemical weapons arsenal remains unclear, so it is difficult to anticipate exactly which agents might be employed at what scale. Assuming for the moment that Russia's arsenal is sufficient to enable large-scale uses, there are still likely other challenges Russia would need to overcome for battlefield use of the weapons. Russian forces may not have the training or expertise needed to operate in a battlefield where chemical weapons are being used without becoming exposed themselves. The relative lack of training being provided to recent Russian conscripts would likely make this problem more acute. Relatedly, Russian chemical and biological units that are trained to respond to and operate in such environments may have seen their members reassigned to other units in the war to help address Russian manpower shortages and may therefore not be operational. That said, Russia's use of chemical weapons on Ukrainians further away from the front lines, against either military or civilian populations, would likely present fewer logistical challenges for Moscow.

Restraining Factors

There are likely several factors that continue to restrain Russia's use of chemical weapons in Ukraine, beyond the potential capacity challenges noted above. Sadly, there is little evidence that the moral implications of chemical weapons use are among these restraining factors given the widespread,

---

[22] Warrick, 2022.

indiscriminate targeting of civilian populations that Russia has undertaken in the conflict. However, five likely restraining factors remain:

1. **Unpredictability of NATO response.** In the past, such as in the Syrian civil war, the United States has identified chemical weapons use as a redline that might prompt its direct intervention in other conflicts. Although the United States and other key NATO members have not made similar explicit statements regarding the Russian use of chemical weapons in Ukraine, the use of these weapons would likely lead to outrage and, depending on the targeting, disgust at Russian behavior that could make assessing NATO reactions unpredictable. Although Russia might be motivated by a desire to shock NATO into curtailing its support for Ukraine, it could also assess a substantial risk of the opposite result and fear that such a result may bring about direct NATO intervention into the war.

2. **Potential loss of status in developing world.** As noted above, Russia has benefited from a relative ambivalence toward its aggression against Ukraine throughout the developing world, which has helped to preserve some measure of its economic and diplomatic standing despite relatively united Western pressure. The use of chemical weapons may well be seen in Moscow as a step that could put this ambivalence at risk and shift a greater number of countries into taking active steps to punish Russia or support Ukraine.

3. **Potential loss of PRC support.** The state whose tacit support Russia needs most urgently to preserve is China, which has acted as Russia's primary economic and diplomatic protector since the start of the conflict. Rhetorically, China is opposed to the use of chemical weapons in the conflict.[23] China may have conveyed either stronger or weaker concerns directly to Russia's leadership. Either way, however, Russia may also be mindful of the fact that China would need to risk its own standing in the developing world should it choose to continue to visibly support Russia after large-scale chemical weap-

---

[23] Ministry of Foreign Affairs of the People's Republic of China, "China's Position on the Political Settlement of the Ukraine Crisis," February 24, 2023.

ons use and that there would likely be a risk that Beijing would be unwilling to do so.

4. **Russia believes it still has a path to achieving its goals in Ukraine.** As discussed above, Moscow likely still believes it has a pathway to achieving its goals in Ukraine absent further escalation, through prevailing in essentially a war of attrition. This perception may be based on accurate information; however, as long as this perception persists, it is likely to restrain Russia from taking on further, riskier gambles.

5. **No acute threats to Russian domestic stability.** Similar to the discussions above, if the Kremlin believes that its control over Russia is stable, it is more likely to also believe that it has time to wait for its current approach to the war to succeed, and it does not need to run undue risks to achieve its goals in Ukraine more quickly. Should Moscow come to believe that regime stability may be under threat, it may be willing to run larger risks to avoid prolonging a war that may threaten the survival of the regime.

Russian Deliberate Nuclear Escalation Options

A deliberate Russian decision to escalate to the use of nuclear weapons in the conflict would have elements of both horizontal and vertical escalation. If used inside Ukraine, nuclear weapons would represent a dramatic vertical escalation of the conflict by Russia. In addition, whether a nuclear detonation occurred inside Ukraine or elsewhere for testing or demonstration purposes, nuclear weapons use would convey an unmissable signal to other countries regarding the steps Russia is willing to take in the conflict that would likely be perceived as a substantial horizontal escalation and threat intended to coerce changes in behavior, such as support for Ukraine, by threatening further nuclear escalation against other states.

We carefully considered several possible nuclear use options for Russia, but we found many of them to be insufficiently plausible. Direct nuclear use against NATO, for example, would invite retaliation that would likely be devastating for the Kremlin, making it difficult to identify a plausible Russian motivation as long as NATO is not directly involved in the conflict. A public demonstration detonation, such as an atmospheric detonation in the Arctic, would be widely condemned as a clearly belligerent act while risking signaling that Russia might hesitate to actually use the weapons in conflict, potentially the worst of both worlds for Moscow. A single battlefield use of a tactical nuclear weapon in Ukraine, meanwhile, would likely have limited operational value while still risking great additional costs for the regime.

We did, however, identify two types of nuclear escalation that Russia could more plausibly undertake in the current conflict: an underground test detonation inside Russia and substantial use of nuclear weapons inside Ukraine.

Russian Underground Test Detonation

Russia has not conducted an acknowledged nuclear test since the collapse of the Soviet Union, with this restraint contributing to a broader international movement to ban nuclear test detonations.[24] In his February 2023 announcement suspending Russian participation in the New Strategic Arms Reduction Treaty (START) agreement, President Putin also indicated Russian willingness to resuming nuclear testing if it believed the United States had done so.[25] As Russia often pre-accuses others of taking steps it intends to take itself, it is quite plausible that Russia could be planning to undertake one or a series of underground nuclear test detonations, which it would publicly announce.

Motivation

Russia's motivation for doing so would likely be twofold. First, and likely less important, Russia may see some value in testing a new warhead design that it could be developing to assess potential effects or reliability issues, although the potential need for such assessments is difficult to assess from the outside.[26] Second, with respect to the conflict in Ukraine, Russia may

---

[24] William Courtney, "Putin Could Escalate with Nuclear Testing," *The Hill*, March 6, 2023.

[25] François Diaz-Maurin, "Russia Suspends New START and Is Ready to Resume Nuclear Testing," *Bulletin of the Atomic Scientists*, February 21, 2023.

[26] Rose Gottemoeller, "Russia Is Updating Their Nuclear Weapons: What Does That Mean for the Rest of Us?" Carnegie Endowment for International Peace, January 29,

view the resumption of nuclear testing as a relatively lower-cost signal than other escalation options discussed above that it can send to NATO to underline the escalatory risks that, in its view, continued NATO support to Ukraine may bring about. It would also have potentially serious implications for global nonproliferation efforts, something that Moscow may come to view as a hostage it can threaten if its demands are not met.

Russia's hope would then likely be that it could fracture NATO cohesion and reduce support for Kyiv by drawing greater attention to nuclear escalation and nonproliferation risks. Such an effort, to be clear, even if successful, would likely take time to shift political decisionmaking in key NATO members and then in turn to affect Ukrainian capabilities, and therefore it is not a plausible, or at least not a plausibly useful, response to an acute battlefield setback Russia may face in Ukraine. But it could be part of a broader Russian strategy to raise the apparent stakes of the conflict for NATO and, in doing so, reduce support for Ukraine.

Capability to Execute

Although difficult to assess with certainty in the public domain, and given that nuclear inspections under New START have not occurred since March 2020, Russia likely has the ability to conduct underground nuclear testing.[27] Doing so would violate Russia's commitments under the Comprehensive Test Ban Treaty (CTBT), which it ratified in 1996 but which has not yet entered into force (although its ratification does bind Russia to take no actions to undermine the treaty). Given Moscow has been systematically withdrawing from or violating key arms control treaties for some time, Russia's international legal commitments would seem to represent no substantial barrier to such a decision.[28]

Restraining Factors

There are likely at least six main factors that have inhibited any deliberate Russian decisions to escalate:

2020; Cheryl Rofer, "Nuclear Tests May Be Back on Moscow's Agenda," *Foreign Policy*, May 15, 2023.

[27] Shannon Bugos, "Russia Further Pauses New START Inspections," *Arms Control Today*, September 2022.

[28] Courtney, 2023.

1. **Indirect linkage to the war in Ukraine.** Russian strategic assets inside Russia have not been threatened by the war in Ukraine. Therefore, there appears to be no plausible defensive need for Russia to assess or enhance the reliability of its nuclear forces. The lack of such a linkage would not necessarily prevent Russia from taking this step, but it would help to ensure that the step was seen by others as aggressive and likely would increase other costs that Russia may expect to face in response.

2. **Potential loss of status in developing world.** As discussed earlier about the use of chemical weapons, Russia's resumption of nuclear testing in what would likely be seen as a clearly aggressive context would put at risk the relative ambivalence of much of the developing world toward Russia's invasion of Ukraine. Russia may be hesitant to risk shifting broader international opinion further against itself, particularly if the benefits of doing so are less than certain.

3. **Potential loss of PRC support.** Russia may be particularly hesitant to risk continued PRC economic and diplomatic support if it assesses that this support may be at risk following a resumption of nuclear testing. China has been a supporter of both the CTBT and broader nuclear nonproliferation efforts and would likely prefer that Russia not take this action.[29] How China would ultimately balance its nuclear concerns and its strategic investments in the survival of the Putin regime in Russia is unclear, but if that is also unclear to the Kremlin, then it may act as a brake on Russian actions.

4. **Uncertainty about U.S. and NATO reactions.** Russia's motivation for resuming nuclear testing would likely be primarily to change decisionmaking in key NATO members and reduce the support they provide to Ukraine. Although this is one plausible reaction to the resumption of Russian nuclear testing, so too is greater anger and determination not to give in to nuclear blackmail, which could in turn harden convictions inside NATO that Russia must be defeated in Ukraine. Unless Russia develops a clear assessment that the

---

[29] "Chinese Envoy Pledges Efforts to Bring CTBT Into Force," Xinhua, September 28, 2021.

former reaction is more likely than the latter, this factor would likely restrain Russia from taking this step.

5. **Russia believes it still has a path to achieving its goals in Ukraine.** As discussed above, Moscow likely still believes it has a pathway to achieving its goals in Ukraine absent further escalation, through prevailing in essentially a war of attrition. This perception may or may not be based on accurate information; however, as long as it persists, it is likely to restrain Russia from taking on further, riskier gambles.

6. **No acute threats to Russian domestic stability.** Similar to the discussions above, if the Kremlin believes that its control over Russia is stable, it is more likely to also believe that it has time to wait for its current approach to the war to succeed, and it does not need to run undue risks to achieve its goals in Ukraine more quickly. Should Moscow come to believe that regime stability may be under threat, it may be willing to run larger risks to avoid prolonging a war that may threaten the survival of the regime.

Substantial Russian Nuclear Use in Ukraine

The final escalation possibility we consider would involve Russian use of nuclear weapons inside Ukraine. The most plausible of these scenarios, in our view, would involve a Russian decision to use nuclear weapons in response to rapid or anticipated catastrophic losses in the Russian military position in Ukraine. Such a use would most plausibly occur on a compressed timeline, in response to an apparently urgent threat to Russian positions that did not appear to allow time for other options to be effective. Time pressures also tend to lead to more emotional, potentially irrational decisions, which has long been of concern to scholars of nuclear deterrence. By contrast, slower-moving Russian losses that allowed time for retreat and the preservation of Russian forces and future military options would be less likely to lead to a decision to cross the nuclear threshold.

The precise number or type of nuclear weapons that Russia could consider using in such circumstances could vary widely, but there are reasons to believe that it would likely not limit itself to a single detonation. The use of a single tactical nuclear device with a smaller yield against Ukrainian forces, for example, may have comparatively limited battlefield effects, given the effects radius of such a weapon and dispersed Ukrainian forces. Should Russia decide to be the first state to cross the nuclear threshold since 1945, it may therefore be more likely to use substantial numbers of such weapons to be more certain of achieving its objectives. Should Russia decide to use nuclear weapons for battlefield effect and, at the same time, assess that a single tactical nuclear detonation would not be effective in stopping a large-scale Ukrainian advance, it may decide that a dozen or two dozen such detonations would, and it may not assess that the costs it would face as a result would differ substantially. Russia may also consider the use of larger-yield, strategic nuclear weapons in the event of a rapid collapse in its forces, because these weapons are likely kept at a higher state of readiness than its tactical weapons and may therefore be able to be employed more quickly.

Moreover, Russian nuclear use against targets without any immediate battlefield effects cannot be ruled out under circumstances in which Russia fears an imminent threat to the survival of its regime. Although nuclear attacks on the Ukrainian leadership or purely civilian targets would do little to diminish Ukraine's near-term military capabilities, these attacks could serve to convince the United States and NATO that the conflict may be spiraling out of control and that they should push for an immediate ceasefire. Under extreme circumstances, Moscow may thus attempt to use nuclear weapons as an instrument of coercion and terror to achieve effects it is unable to achieve on the battlefield directly. In doing so, Russia would need to be willing to trade off the heightened risk of direct NATO military involvement for the possibility that NATO could instead push for an immediate ceasefire.

Motivation

Russia's motivation for the use of nuclear weapons in the circumstances described above would be to prevent catastrophic Russian battlefield losses sufficient to threaten the survival of the regime. The anticipated losses would need to be severe, constituting a threat to the overall Russian position in Ukraine, and they would likely need to be rapid or imminent and not accumulating losses from a war of attrition. To achieve this goal, as noted above, Russia could decide to use nuclear weapons either as a military instrument to achieve battlefield effects, such as halting a Ukrainian advance, or as an instrument of coercion designed to signal that the war has spiraled or is about to spiral out of control unless the Ukrainian advance is halted.

Capability to Execute

Russia's nuclear forces have been the most consistently funded and prioritized of its military services. Russia has exercised using tactical nuclear weapons in combat and likely has the ability to execute such strikes using a variety of means. The use of strategic nuclear weapons requires both Russian political and military authorization, while the requirements for the use of lower-yield weapons are less clear.[30] In either event, however, given the concentrated nature of power in Russia, it seems highly unlikely that, should Putin decide to use nuclear weapons, any current senior military figure would also refuse to provide his own authorization. As noted above, Russia's higher-yield strategic nuclear weapons are likely kept at a higher state of readiness than its tactical nuclear weapons. In a rapid collapse scenario, this may encourage Russia to consider the use of strategic weapons, unless steps had been taken in advance to increase the readiness of some portion of its tactical nuclear weapons inventory.

Although not necessarily affecting Russia's ability to use a nuclear weapon, it should be noted that Russian ground forces (particularly the Russian ground forces as they stand today) likely have insufficient training regarding how to fight on a nuclear battlefield, which could, in turn, complicate Russian efforts to take tactical advantage of such strikes. But these factors would not necessarily restrain Russia from executing these strikes if its priority was to halt or destroy Ukrainian forces or to highlight the danger and unpredictability of allowing the conflict to continue rather than to enable a Russian advance.

Restraining Factors

There are several factors that are likely restraining Russia's use of nuclear weapons today. Perhaps the most critical of these is reflected in the scenario for such use that we outline above, in which Russia fears an imminent collapse in its military position. Such a situation would mean that Russia may no longer view itself as having an alternative path to achieving its goals in

---

[30] Kristin Ven Bruusgaard, "How Russia Decides to Go Nuclear," *Foreign Affairs*, February 6, 2023.

the war (and as a result avoiding severe threats to regime security), a key restraining condition noted for many of the other escalation options discussed earlier. The use of nuclear weapons in Ukraine would likely come about only under conditions in which Russia feared precisely that it may face a choice between nuclear use and defeat. In addition, the scenario posits that Russia is more likely to use nuclear weapons if forced to decide on how to avoid a military collapse quickly. More-gradual Russian losses that accumulate over time would provide (1) no clear moment in time or geographic location where the potential battlefield benefits of nuclear use would outweigh the other costs and (2) more time for Russian decisionmakers to come to more carefully considered decisions. Beyond these core conditions, three other factors would be likely to restrain Russian battlefield nuclear use even were it to face a scenario like the one we describe above:

1. **The possibility of NATO entry into the war.** Although maintaining a policy of strategic ambiguity, the United States and NATO have signaled that Russian use of nuclear weapons would cause them to rethink their approach to the war.[31] In particular, NATO appears to have signaled the possibility that Russian nuclear use in the conflict could precipitate direct U.S. or NATO conventional intervention in the conflict.[32] NATO intervention in the conflict could quite plausibly erase any potential battlefield gains Russia sought to achieve through nuclear use (should Russia be seeking battlefield advantage rather than coercive signaling) and might lead to more-comprehensive losses of Russian forces than were threatened by a Ukrainian advance alone. If Russia perceives these NATO threats to intervene more forcefully in the conflict in response to Russian nuclear use as credible, and more likely than a NATO push for an immediate ceasefire, then these perceptions would likely have a restraining effect on Russian decisionmaking. Should NATO's approach to this issue shift, however, possibly because of changes

---

[31] "Biden Warns Putin on Use of WMDs: 'Don't, Don't, Don't,'" Voice of America, September 17, 2022.

[32] Sabine Siebold and Phil Stewart, "Russian Nuclear Strike Likely to Provoke 'Physical Response,' NATO Official Says," Reuters, October 12, 2022.

in government in key NATO member states or degradations in Alliance cohesion, then Russian concerns for this risk could become attenuated. In addition, it is important to note that, should Russia come to believe that NATO's direct intervention in the conflict will occur regardless of its decisions regarding nuclear use, then this factor would likely remove any restraining effect that fears of a future NATO intervention might otherwise have.

2. **The possible loss of PRC support.** Although Russia would no doubt face widespread international condemnation following the use of nuclear weapons in Ukraine, faced with an acute military collapse, its concerns over its longer-term reputation or diplomatic position may be set to one side. What the Kremlin may not feel it can ignore, however, is the reaction of Beijing. If China were to signal to Russia that it were willing to impose sanctions or otherwise economically and diplomatically isolate the Kremlin, this action could raise the possibility that even if Russia were successful in averting a near-term battlefield collapse, it would then face a much more challenging aftermath, with potentially greater risks to regime stability. It is not clear what signals Beijing may have sent Moscow on this issue or what Russia believes China's response would be in this eventuality. Russia may find any threats from China to abandon Moscow not to be credible given how losing its relationship with Russia would affect China's own long-term strategic competition with the United States. But China is likely the only one of Russia's partners that has sufficient leverage over Moscow to change Russia's calculus on nuclear use, should it choose to do so.

3. **Potential loss of regime legitimacy.** Breaking the nuclear taboo by becoming the first state to use nuclear weapons in war since 1945 would amplify a series of longer-term risks for the Russian regime. Although the effects of these risks would be felt more gradually (and therefore may not be sufficient to dissuade Russian nuclear use to stave off more-acute perceived threats to regime survival), they still represent important factors in helping to raise the bar for Russian nuclear use in the first place: for example, using nuclear weapons in an aggressive war against a neighboring state risks delegitimizing the regime, potentially domestically but more likely in the inter-

national community. This could in turn make cooperation with or defense of the Russian regime politically impossible for most states, with any number of possible downstream effects, ranging from sharp declines in trade or investment from the developing world to threats to the Russian place on the Security Council at the United Nations. As noted above, the reaction of China would likely be important to determining the scale and scope of these effects, but should Beijing decide to abandon Moscow, it could lead to several further negative effects for the Kremlin that would likely weigh on its decision.

Ukrainian or NATO Deliberate Escalation Options

Russia remains the actor with the greatest potential to pursue deliberate escalation in the conflict. NATO has immense potential capabilities that it could bring to bear in the conflict but also a demonstrated strong desire to avoid doing so. Ukraine, meanwhile, is similarly—if not more—motivated to do everything in its power to win the conflict, but it has limited options to do so that would go beyond its current efforts. We identified one main plausible option by which Ukraine could intentionally escalate the conflict, under certain circumstances, discussed in the following sections. Although we also carefully considered potential NATO intentional escalation scenarios, those we identified appeared less plausible than the other options considered in this chapter.[33]

---

[33] It should be noted that NATO has escalated its role in the conflict on multiple occasions when it has expanded the nature or scale of the assistance that it has provided to Ukraine. However, NATO has been extremely cautious to do so only incrementally, such that no individual change in assistance on its own has represented a dramatic change in the conflict, likely reducing Russian incentives to escalate in response at any particular moment. NATO could depart from this pattern in the future and begin to provide capabilities that would mark a radical departure from past patterns, although NATO's motivations for doing so as long as Ukraine is performing well on the battlefield are unclear. The possibility of Ukrainian reversals on the battlefield raises another possible scenario that could cause NATO to revisit its refusal to become directly involved in the war: a renewed direct threat to Kyiv and the Zelenskyy administration itself. Since the start of the war, Ukraine has built extensive political, diplomatic, and military links throughout the Alliance, and public support for Ukraine in most Alliance members has been robust and durable. NATO members have provided Ukraine with more than $100 billion in assistance since the start of the war, a staggering sum in comparison with past security

Expansion of Ukrainian Strikes Inside Russia

As of June 2023, Ukraine has undertaken some limited retaliatory strikes inside Russian territory. These strikes—undertaken both by the Ukrainian military and by other associated groups—have primarily relied on armed UASs to target military bases or symbolic targets such as Moscow far from the front lines, although there have also been limited ground attacks along the Russia-Ukraine border.[34] These strikes to date have been limited not only in number but in the types of weapons used in them. The United States and other key NATO allies have consistently told Ukraine that they expect the weapons they are providing to Kyiv not to be used for attacks inside Russia, out of concerns for the risks of escalation that such strikes might raise.[35] Although Ukraine's adherence to this rule may have been bent at the margins, this condition overall does appear to have been followed and has likely limited the capabilities Ukraine has put toward strikes inside Russia.[36]

That said, further expansion of Ukrainian strikes inside Russia is plausible in at least three possible ways. First, Ukraine could expand the number and frequency of UAS strikes inside Russian territory dramatically. Ukraine sources its UAS fleet primarily from non-NATO sources and therefore may not feel constrained by NATO concerns regarding direct attacks on Rus-

---

cooperation efforts. The risk of similar threats to Ukraine's existence as an independent state as those it faced in February 2022 appear remote. But should battlefield conditions change radically, potentially as a result of Russian escalation decisions, and should Kyiv and the Zelenskyy administration again be threatened directly, it is plausible that NATO could then consider more escalatory steps. Given the overall implausibility of that scenario arising for the foreseeable future, however, we do not assess it in greater detail here (see Jonathan Masters and Will Merrow, "How Much Aid Has the U.S. Sent Ukraine? Here Are Six Charts," Council on Foreign Relations, May 19, 2023).

[34] Andrew E. Kramer, Michael Schwirtz, and Marc Santora, "Ukraine Targets Bases Deep in Russia, Showing Expanded Reach," *New York Times*, December 5, 2022; Julian E. Barnes, Adam Entous, Eric Schmitt and Anton Troianovski, "Ukrainians Were Likely Behind Kremlin Drone Attack, U.S. Officials Say," *New York Times*, May 24, 2023; Andrew E. Kramer, Valerie Hopkins, and Michael Schwirtz, "Anti-Kremlin Fighters Take War to Russian Territory for a Second Day," *New York Times*, May 23, 2023.

[35] Idrees Ali and Phil Stewart, "Ukraine Shouldn't Use US Weaponry Inside Russia, US General Says," Reuters, May 25, 2023.

[36] Riley Mellen, "Pro-Ukraine Forces Appear to Have Used U.S.-Made Armored Vehicles in Incursion into Russia," *New York Times*, May 23, 2023.

sian territory using these capabilities.[37] Second, Ukraine could alter the targets of the attacks it undertakes. Although these targets have included such sensitive locations as Russian airbases and the capital city, more-concerted efforts to attack Russian leadership directly—something that Russia alleges Ukraine is doing but for which there is no current public evidence—would likely represent an escalation. Third, Ukraine could decide to contravene NATO restrictions on the use of more-advanced weapons, essentially forcing NATO members to make an unpalatable choice between reducing or eliminating assistance to Kyiv or accepting (and therefore being seen by Moscow to tacitly support) such an escalation. For example, the recently provided Storm Shadow cruise missiles could be employed for more-destructive strikes inside Russian territory, although they lack the range to reach many sensitive targets, such as Moscow.[38]

Motivation

Ukraine has suffered tremendously as a result of the Russian invasion and, in particular, the ongoing Russian long-range strike campaign against Ukrainian critical infrastructure and population centers. Part of Ukraine's motivation for escalating its strikes against targets inside Russia would likely be retaliatory. But Ukraine may also view expanding such strikes as a means of increasing costs, including domestic political pressures, on the Kremlin to end its invasion. Ukraine may also see possible military advantages in its ability to strike Russian logistics or transport nodes that may affect the capabilities that Russia is able to transfer to Ukraine, particularly if such strikes could be timed to a critical Ukrainian offensive.

Capability to Execute

Ukraine has demonstrated a limited capacity to undertake UAS strikes against targets deep inside Russia, although the kinetic effects of those strikes to date have been limited. Russia, meanwhile, has also demonstrated an

---

[37] Adam Lowther and Mahbube K. Siddiki, "Combat Drones in Ukraine," *Air and Space Operations Review*, Vol. 1, No. 4, Winter 2022.

[38] Dan Sabbagh and Luke Harding, "UK Sending Long-Range Storm Shadow Missiles to Ukraine, Says Defence Minister," *The Guardian*, May 11, 2023.

ability to interdict such strikes using both physical and electronic means.[39] However, if Ukraine is willing to accept that an individual UAS will be frequently interdicted or ineffective and attempt to overcome these issues by increasing the number of such strikes, it likely has the ability to expand the number of successful attacks it carries out. However, it should be noted that Ukraine makes heavy use of its UAS capabilities for its main operations against Russian forces inside its territory. Sharply increasing the resources put toward strikes against targets inside Russia would presumably come at some cost with respect to these operations. Ukraine could also attempt to use its manned aircraft for longer-range strikes inside Russia, although the ability of these platforms to avoid Russian air defense capabilities in the way that smaller UASs have proven able to is unclear.

Restraining Factors

There are likely at least three main factors that have inhibited Ukraine from undertaking more-expansive strikes against targets inside Russia to date:

1. **More-pressing military needs.** Ukraine has been stretched to the limit in its efforts to evict invading Russian forces from its territory. Russian troops remain in possession of substantial parts of Ukrainian territory, including those occupied both before and after February 2022. Retaking captured Ukrainian territory has been the overriding military priority for Kyiv. Strikes deep inside Russian territory, at least at the scale and intensity of which Kyiv is capable, are likely to have only limited (if any) effects on this campaign. Although Ukraine may decide that investing more resources in strikes inside Russia and thereby increasing political costs for the Kremlin may be worthwhile, such strikes still would largely represent a second line of effort from the main military campaign. Given the priority that Ukraine likely attaches to the success of its ground campaign, it may be hesitant to devote substantial resources to other efforts unless the ground campaign were to stabilize or bog down and Kyiv begins to assess that further advances or losses have become less

---

[39] "Moscow Drone Attack Exposes Russia's Vulnerabilities, Fuels Criticism of Military," Associated Press, May 30, 2023.

likely with both sides dug into defensive positions. If such a situation does occur, Kyiv may become more open to alternative options for increasing pressure on Russia to withdraw.

2. **Risks of leadership targeting.** Ukraine is likely not particularly concerned over the possibility that Russia may respond in kind to Ukrainian strikes on most targets inside Russia, given Russia's virtually unrestrained targeting of both military and civilian targets throughout Ukraine over the past several months. There is simply not much left for Ukraine to fear from Russia in this regard given what it has already experienced. One possible exception, however, could be with respect to Ukrainian strikes on the Russian leadership itself. Although Russia was quick to publicly claim that Ukrainian UAS strikes on Moscow in early May 2023 were an attempt on Putin's life, this is not, frankly, a plausible interpretation of the strike given the weapons involved.[40] But future Ukrainian strikes could more plausibly be aimed at the Russian leadership itself, either through attacking less protected locations than the Kremlin or by assigning greater resources to the attack. Such an effort, whether successful or not, could lead to an escalatory response by Russia, such as a more concerted effort to kill the Ukrainian leadership using a barrage of long-range strikes at the center of Kyiv designed to overwhelm Ukrainian air defenses. Although Moscow did apparently attempt to capture or assassinate Zelenskyy in the early days of the war, at least publicly, it does not appear to have prioritized similar actions later in the conflict.[41] That said, little is publicly known about the degree to which such concerns might restrain Ukraine from targeting Russia's leadership, and the operational challenges of doing so successfully are likely the greater restraining factor for Kyiv regardless.

3. **Potential reduction in NATO support.** NATO and particularly the United States have consistently emphasized their desire to keep

---

[40] Will Vernon and Thomas Spender, "Kremlin Drone: Zelensky Denies Ukraine Attacked Putin or Moscow," BBC News, May 3, 2023.

[41] Timothy Bella, "Assassination Plot Against Zelensky Foiled and Unit Sent to Kill Him 'Destroyed,' Ukraine Says," *Washington Post*, March 2, 2022.

the fighting in this war contained inside Ukraine's borders. This goal can be seen clearly in the promises that NATO countries have extracted from Ukraine not to use the weapons they have provided to Kyiv for strikes on Russia, but it is also likely that this extends to the disapproval of Ukraine using its own capabilities for similar strikes. Therefore, Kyiv might believe that a Ukrainian decision to give greater priority to such strikes would risk a reduction in the extensive support being provided to it by NATO, which it now depends almost entirely on for its battlefield success. NATO countries, including the United States, could change the messages they are sending to Kyiv on this issue should they choose to do so, if for example they no longer assess that such strikes would risk further Russian escalation. But absent a change in policy from NATO, this factor seems likely to be among the main issues restraining more-intensive Ukrainian strikes inside Russia.

Summary

This chapter illustrates several types of deliberate escalation that could plausibly occur in the ongoing war in Ukraine, as summarized in Table 3.1.

As our discussion above of each escalation option indicates, however, several factors affect the likelihood of states deciding to pursue these options under different circumstances. Both the capability to execute each escalation option and the balance between the motivation to undertake the option and the factors that may further restrain Russia and Ukraine from doing so vary widely. Although only an illustrative approximation, Figure 3.1 summarizes the relative likelihood of the deliberate escalation options discussed above as of this writing.

We do not observe an imminent risk that any of these deliberate escalation pathways is about to be undertaken, although some—such as an increase in Ukrainian attacks inside Russia or a Russian nuclear test detonation—do appear to be more likely than others as of this writing. This assessment of the approximate likelihood of different options, however, is highly dependent on the specific circumstances of the conflict and how each option may affect the motivations and restraining factors noted above. As an alterna-

TABLE 3.1

Plausible Deliberate Escalation Options in Ongoing War in Ukraine

Option	Motivation	Ability to Execute	Restraining Factors
Limited Russian attack against NATO in Europe	Coerce NATO member states to limit or cease support to Ukraine	Varies depending on scale and nature of attack	• Does not view direct NATO intervention as inevitable • Anticipates that NATO's response would be devastating • Ukrainian use of U.S.-NATO supplied military capabilities against Russian territory is restricted • Increase in NATO assistance has been gradual • Belief it can win a war of attrition • No acute threats to Russian domestic stability
Russia provokes out-of-area crisis	Shift U.S. and allies attention to reduce support for Ukraine	Challenging to incentivize a state to provoke a crisis unless it was already predisposed	• Russian reluctance to take further risks • Potential for hardening international opposition to Russia
Russia conducts large scale air and missile campaign against Ukraine	Establish some measure of air superiority in skies over Ukraine	Russia may incur serious losses to destroy Ukrainian air defenses but may be able to do so	• Russian desire to preserve its capabilities to deter NATO attack • Difficulty of replacing lost aircraft and pilots • Public and diplomatic reaction to high-profile losses • Belief it can win a war of attrition • No acute threats to Russian domestic stability

Table 3.1—Continued

Option	Motivation	Ability to Execute	Restraining Factors
Russia initiates large-scale use of chemical weapons in Ukraine	Battlefield advantage; break Ukrainian civilian and military morale; motivate NATO members to push Ukraine to negotiations	Size and scope of chemical weapons arsenal unclear; logistical challenges in employment	• Risk of triggering direct NATO intervention • Potential loss of status in developing world • Potential loss of PRC's support • Belief it can win a war of attrition • No acute threats to Russian domestic stability
Russia conducts underground nuclear test	Lower-cost signal to NATO of escalatory risks that continued NATO support entails; threat to nonproliferation efforts to use as leverage	Russia likely has capability to conduct nuclear tests	• No plausible direct link to Ukrainian actions, ensuring that step is viewed as aggressive • Potential loss of status in developing world • Potential loss of PRC's support • Uncertainty about U.S and NATO reactions: reduce support to Ukraine or harden commitment to Russia's defeat • Belief it can win a war of attrition • No acute threats to Russian domestic stability
Russia uses nuclear weapons inside Ukraine	Prevent rapid catastrophic Russian battlefield losses that could threaten the survival of the regime; coerce NATO into pushing for a ceasefire because of escalation fears	Extensive Russian nuclear capabilities; however, tactical weapons kept at lower readiness levels, and Russian ground forces likely ill-prepared to operate on nuclear battlefield	• Possibility of NATO entry into the war • Potential loss of PRC support • Potential loss of regime's legitimacy

Table 3.1—Continued

Option	Motivation	Ability to Execute	Restraining Factors
Ukraine expands its strikes inside Russia	Increase domestic political costs for Russian leadership, hamper Russia's military activities by striking logistics or command and control centers	Some demonstrated capability to execute UAS strikes. Expanding campaign likely possible if willing to accept losses, trade-offs with frontline operations.	• Strikes might not be effective • More pressing military needs for their forces • Russia might target Ukrainian leadership in response • NATO might reduce its support if weapons they have provided are used to strike inside Russia

tive, the likelihood of different deliberate escalation options in a scenario in which Russia faces an imminent military collapse in Ukraine, including the likely destruction or capture of most major Russian forces in the country, could look like quite different, as shown in Figure 3.2.

In such a scenario, some escalation options would become less likely, including a limited Russian attack on NATO or Russian attempts to provoke an out-of-area crisis, because of their inability to quickly improve Russia's military position. But other options that Russia has previously avoided but could assess to be effective as a last-ditch attempt to rescue the military situation, such as nuclear or chemical weapons use, could increase in likelihood. Even in such a circumstance, Russia may well avoid such highly consequential actions for the reasons discussed above. But the increased risk of such actions in these circumstances underlines the importance of thinking through in advance how policymakers might respond and what steps they can take to further reduce their likelihood.

FIGURE 3.1

Illustrative Summary of Likelihood of Deliberate Escalation Options (July 2023)

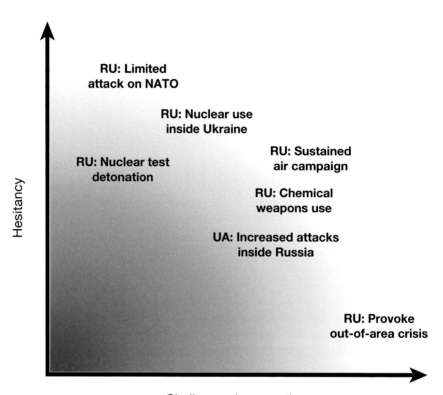

Challenges in execution

NOTE: RU = Russia; UA = Ukraine. The horizontal axis summarizes the challenges Russia or Ukraine would face in executing this option, with more-executable options to the left and less-executable options to the right. The vertical axis summarizes the likely degree of Russian or Ukrainian hesitancy to attempt the option, taking into account both their motivations to do so and the other restraining factors that may affect their decisions to do so, as discussed earlier in the chapter. Options that are higher in the figure are those that Russia or Ukraine would be more hesitant to attempt, and options that are lower in the figure are those that these states would be less hesitant to attempt. Taking these two dimensions together, the closer an option is to the bottom-left of the figure, the more likely we assess that it might occur under these circumstances.

FIGURE 3.2

Illustrative Summary of Likelihood of Deliberate Escalation Options (Russian Collapse Scenario)

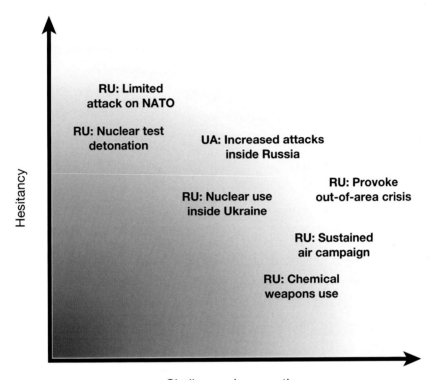

Challenges in execution

NOTE: RU = Russia; UA = Ukraine.

CHAPTER 4

Conclusions and Implications

Any assessment of the risk of Russian escalation in the ongoing conflict in Ukraine should be approached with humility. Prior to the war, the West had numerous insights into how the Russian military as an institution was likely to approach escalation decisions. However, in the current conflict, Putin has adopted an increasingly centralized, and apparently personalized, decision-making process in which the military may have limited influence or input into key decisions. Russian behavior in the conflict to date does provide information on Putin's perceptions and reactions, but there are clear limits on what we can draw from such information in anticipating future Russian escalation decisions.

This is, in large part, because the current conflict—or any prior conflict in which Russia has been involved under Putin—has yet to evolve to a point at which Russian regime security or other vital interests are acutely threatened. Therefore, we have no direct information regarding how Putin may respond under these circumstances, should they arise in the current conflict. Beyond observing Russian behavior in the less regime-threatening circumstances of the conflict to date, we can also develop baseline expectations regarding how state leaders tend to behave in such perilous situations from the broader international relations literature, as discussed in the preceding chapters. However, Russia under Putin may ultimately prove to be an exception, or not, to such rules.

Therefore, we should not approach this topic with a high degree of confidence in being able to anticipate Putin's reactions to perceived threats to the security of his regime, should the conflict in Ukraine evolve to do so. We argue in this report that this lack of confidence in our understanding of Russian escalation decisions under such circumstances should breed caution. Analyses that argue alternately that Russian nuclear use is either certain or can be essentially set to one side, for example, to our mind give insufficient weight to the difficulties of anticipating such a reaction.[1]

U.S. and NATO policymakers must still make decisions regarding how to approach the conflict despite these uncertainties. Western officials have multiple goals in the conflict beyond limiting Russian escalation: Most notably, supporting Ukraine's defense, maintaining Alliance cohesion, punishing Russian aggression, and lacking clarity regarding Russian escalation calculations do not make these other goals less important. Identifying and balancing potential trade-offs among U.S. and NATO goals for the conflict is likely to remain an inexact and messy process.

The purpose of this report is to better inform these decisions by assessing what can be learned from Russian behavior in the conflict to date and how this may affect the likelihood of different escalation pathways going forward. The process of researching and writing this report has generated numerous insights and implications, which we summarize in the following sections. However, on their own, these findings do not resolve policy questions regarding which U.S. goals to prioritize and how. Our hope is for debates regarding these questions to better informed as a result of this work, but we do not aim to settle them.

Learning from Russian Escalation Decisions in the Conflict to Date

Immediately following Russia's invasion of Ukraine, the United States and its NATO allies were consumed with finding a balance between responding to Russian aggression and avoiding steps that would escalate the conflict to a direct Russia-NATO war. Russia and the West both entered the early stages of the war with several misperceptions and faulty assumptions that played a significant role in shaping both sides' decisionmaking on escalation. By overestimating its capabilities and prospects for success while underestimating Ukrainian will to resist and NATO cohesion, Russia

---

[1] Kevin Ryan, "Why Putin Will Use Nuclear Weapons in Ukraine," Russia Matters, May 17, 2023; Phil Stewart and Idrees Ali, "Russia 'Very Unlikely' to Use Nuclear Weapons, US Intel Chief," Reuters, May 4, 2023.

appeared to have devoted little effort before the war to developing viable escalatory courses of action. Furthermore, any Western threats to punish Russia or support Ukraine prior to the invasion were perceived to be of lower cost or risk, given Russian assessments of a quick victory. Using the Kremlin's assessment that it could obtain its objectives quickly, with limited external interference and at limited cost, it most likely concluded that additional, more escalatory courses of action would not be necessary. Perhaps as a result, Russia's responses to and efforts to employ escalatory courses of action since the failure of the initial attempts to seize Kyiv have appeared to be halting and incomplete.

That said, Russia has pursued several escalatory measures in the conflict, including horizontal escalation (from the shutoff of gas exports to Europe to the attempts to prevent Ukrainian grain shipments badly needed throughout the developing world) and vertical escalation (e.g., expanded bombing campaign and human rights abuses against civilian targets inside Ukraine). Although none of these have had the desired effect of altering Ukrainian or NATO behavior in the ways that Putin and his inner circle appear to have sought, they do reflect a Kremlin that is actively exploring and perhaps testing the reactions to different escalation options.

Although Russia has pursued escalation in the conflict at numerous points, there have also been several factors that appear to have restrained the Kremlin from going further, particularly in the military domain. First, Russia's behavior to date suggests an acute fear of NATO's military capabilities. This likely has become more salient over time due to Russia's accumulating losses and the current state of its military. Second, Russia is likely still sensitive to international reactions, at least from its more established partners, to its prosecution of the war. This sensitivity has probably forced the Kremlin to moderate its approach as a result, as seen by its intermittent willingness to allow Ukrainian grain exports and its courting of PRC support for the conflict. However, these factors on their own do not necessarily preclude Russia from pursuing additional escalatory options in the future, and in at least one instance these factors could also increase the risk of escalation under different circumstances. For instance, Russia's acute concern over the potential for a NATO first strike against Russian command and control systems, including leadership targets, may instill in Russia's leaders a perceived need to "go first" should they come to believe that such a strike is imminent.

The third factor that appears to be restraining further Russian escalation to date is the perception in the Kremlin that taking further risks may not yet be necessary. Although the Wagner mutiny for the first time raises this specter, the conflict has yet to present acute threats to the stability of the current Russian regime. This factor, in turn, has allowed the Kremlin more time to see whether its current strategy will eventually wear down Ukrainian resistance and NATO cohesion. As long as Russia can endure its own extensive costs in the conflict, and its domestic challenges do not increase, it may still believe that it will eventually prevail without the need to run greater escalation risks.

The greatest concern we identified in this report is what Russia might decide to do if events on the battlefield or inside Russia convince the Russian leadership that they are wrong in this assessment and that escalation is required to avoid acute threats to the survival of the regime. Major Russian escalation decisions in the past, including the expansion of the critical infrastructure bombing campaign in fall 2022 and the June 2023 destruction of the Kakhovka Dam occurred in conjunction with recent or anticipated Ukrainian offensives that threatened Russia's forces and position in Ukraine. But these comparatively limited examples of Russian escalation have come in response to non-existential threats to the regime in Moscow. How Russia might respond to more acute threats, should the conflict present them, remains unknown.

Russia is not the only actor that may pursue deliberate escalation in the conflict. Ukraine has strong military and political incentives to try to impose greater costs on Russia, particularly as Russia continues to target Ukrainian population centers. To date, although Ukraine has undertaken several attacks on targets inside Russia, the scale and effects of these attacks have been quite limited. These limitations likely reflect both the enormous operational demands of Ukrainian operations to expel Russian forces from Ukrainian territory and the pressure from the United States and other key NATO allies to refrain from such attacks. NATO's preferences not to widen the war into Russian territory are driven by its own concerns over the escalation risks that might result. These preferences have been expressed both in promises extracted from Ukraine not to use NATO-provided capabilities in these attacks and in NATO's caution in not providing Ukraine with weapons with sufficient range to be used for strikes on Moscow or Russian leadership targets, with the latter factor likely being the more effective one in limiting escalation risks over the long term. Should Ukraine assess that putting greater focus on strikes inside Russia is necessary to either win the war or avoid defeat, it may not be realistic to expect that any NATO pressure or prior promises to avoid such strikes would be effective.

U.S. and NATO Efforts to Manage Escalation Risks

Improving our understanding of when and why Russia may decide to escalate in the future, including potentially to nuclear use, requires acknowledging that past Western understandings of Russian escalation calculations appear to have been flawed. Prior to the invasion, the United States and Europe viewed Russian escalation, including potentially nuclear use, as highly likely in circumstances similar to those that did ultimately occur in the war, given the stakes involved in the conflict for the Kremlin and the losses Russia has already sustained to date. From both a national and an Alliance perspective, NATO planners focused heavily on not provoking Russia and tailoring responses that would avoid escalatory responses from the Kremlin. To date, most of these concerns with escalation have not come to fruition.

These two observations—fewer than expected cases of Russian escalation and prewar assessments that overestimated Russia's willingness to escalate—could lead a reasonable observer to conclude that the potential for future Russian escalation will follow a similar pattern. One implication of such a conclusion might be to accelerate the speed and expand the scope of lethal aid to Ukraine well beyond the relatively measured, incremental approach taken to this point in the conflict.

Under the current battlefield dynamics of a relative stalemate, such an accelerated approach to supporting Ukraine may have limited short-term escalation risks. However, these dynamics may change if the Kremlin's assessments of the war's trajectory and its prospects for threatening the survival of the regime, possibly by feeding internal instability or rapid and widespread loss of support from Russian elites, were also to change.

Major shocks or surprises (e.g., the rapid deterioration of Russia's military position in Ukraine or sharp degradation of internal stability inside Russia) might prompt the Kremlin to view escalatory options like those described in Chapter 3 as the only viable alternatives to reverse these trends and cause its approach to escalation to depart from what has been observed in the conflict to date.

Most of the escalatory scenarios identified in our brainstorming session and examined earlier in this report assume some type of deliberate escalation. However, inadvertent escalation risks resulting from the behavior of all parties should not be discounted. In any situation involving sustained high-intensity, high-stakes warfare with a nuclear power, the risk of inadvertent escalation will reside in the background. The types of activities that could lead to inadvertent escalation, many of which are an integral part of both sides' war efforts (e.g., long-range strikes on targets where accuracy or targeting information may be flawed), will likely continue to pose such risks for the duration of the war.

The Problem of Nuclear Escalation

As the war continues, increased losses of Russian personnel and capabilities are likely to make conventional military escalation options less effective or less appealing to Russian decisionmakers. The expenditure of long-range precision weapons, the threat to delivery platforms, and the threat of NATO retaliation all are likely to increasingly limit Russia's conventional escalation options as the conflict lengthens. For this reason, chemical or nuclear escalation options against Ukraine may become comparatively more attractive to Putin and his inner circle if they are in a position in which they are evaluating options to respond to a perceived threat to regime security.

In such circumstances, there are in principle many possible ways in which Russia could employ nuclear weapons. Technical and operational issues involved in employing these weapons would likely in practice limit some of these options. The inexperience and lack of training of current Russian ground forces in operating in a nuclear battlefield and the practical limitations regarding the time needed to employ tactical nuclear weapons, at least at current readiness levels, could constrain the scenarios in which

Russia would believe that using nuclear weapons would generate battle-field advantages. Identifying targeting options that could halt a Ukrainian advance without also adversely affecting Russian forces may be difficult if those forces are already in close proximity. For these and other reasons, Russia likely has a very high bar to battlefield nuclear use in Ukraine.

However, Russia may also use nuclear weapons inside Ukraine not only or primarily for battlefield effects but to signal to both Ukraine and NATO that the risks of escalation to general nuclear war have become acute if the battlefield situation is not stabilized. In our brainstorming sessions, it was unclear whether either of these options would deliver the operational or psychological impact that Russia might seek to change either Ukrainian or NATO behavior and effectively coerce a ceasefire. And the risks to the Kremlin from using nuclear weapons would be enormous, likely increasing the long-term potential for regime abandonment and collapse.

But a desperate situation for Russian forces inside Ukraine that in turn appears to threaten the political survival of the regime could still lead the Kremlin to view nuclear use as the best of a series of bad options. Ultimately, should Russia decide to use nuclear weapons inside Ukraine, it may be rela-tively unrestrained in their employment. For instance, Putin may decide to use as many tactical nuclear weapons as are needed to achieve his near-term objectives (e.g., preventing a military collapse or coercing a ceasefire), or he may decide to use strategic nuclear weapons that can be employed more quickly. Although we have little direct insight into how Putin perceives this issue, it could be a mistake to assume that, having decided to use nuclear weapons, Russia would then also decide to be restrained in the number or types of weapons it employed. Russia's leadership may not perceive that the costs and risks associated with using a small number or size of nuclear weapons against Ukraine would be dramatically different from those asso-ciated with using a larger number or size of such weapons, particularly if the Kremlin believed that the latter would achieve Russian battlefield objectives while the former may not.

Implications for U.S. and NATO Policymakers

This report highlights several implications for U.S. and NATO policymakers in the war in Ukraine. First, maintaining Alliance cohesion regarding what the escalation risks are and which risks are desirable to take on as a result of efforts to support Ukraine and punish Russia is an essential critical factor both in long-term Ukrainian military success and in helping to deter Russian horizontal escalation. Public disagreement within the Alliance regarding the management of escalation risks could feed Russian perceptions that efforts to coerce NATO by threatening further escalation may have a greater chance of success.

Second, the priority that NATO policymakers should therefore place on maintaining Alliance cohesion regarding escalation management may affect other policy decisions, including the extent and pace of military support provided to Ukraine. Should the United States or another key NATO member decide to provide capabilities to Ukraine that lack consensus within the Alliance because of allied perceptions of their escalatory risk, and should such disagreements became public, it could have negative effects on Russian perceptions of the likelihood that NATO would respond in a unified, cohesive manner to escalatory options the Kremlin might be considering. Therefore, such a policy would risk trading off potential short-term battlefield gains for Ukraine against increased horizontal escalation risks, as Russia would be (1) more incentivized to attempt to interdict or coerce an end to such support and (2) potentially more optimistic that such efforts could succeed.

That said, we do not have clear public information regarding the extent to which Alliance cohesion considerations may be continuing to slow the pace of NATO assistance to Ukraine, although disagreements over these issues were apparent at earlier stages of the conflict.[2] Certainly the United States' own escalation concerns and assessments of Ukraine's ability to absorb the assistance and of the relative military utility of more-advanced capabilities also play a role.[3] It is also possible, however, that to maintain

---

[2] Hans von der Burchard, "Germany Approves Tank Sales to Ukraine, Bowing to Pressure," *Politico*, April 26, 2022.

[3] Lara Seligman, "How Biden Got to Yes on F-16s and Ukraine," *Politico*, May 22, 2023.

Alliance cohesion, the United States is expressing greater doubts regarding the advisability of providing certain assistance on behalf of allies that may be more reticent to make such arguments publicly themselves. This appears to be the current dynamic regarding consideration of future Ukrainian membership in NATO, for example, in which U.S. public discouragement likely reflects broader hesitation among other European alliance members that may face greater political challenges in expressing these sentiments.[4] For the purposes of this report, we would note that Alliance cohesion is likely to remain an important factor in helping to deter Russian escalation and should therefore be balanced against operational assessments of the value that expanded assistance could provide to Ukraine.

Third, the incremental approach taken thus far by the United States and its allies in providing assistance to Ukraine may have contributed to limiting Russian escalation, but this strategy may also work against Ukraine as Russia continues to mobilize and put new forces in the field and Ukrainian losses continue to increase. As noted in previous sections, Putin appears to believe that Russia has time on its side, meaning it has a long-term resource advantage that will enable it to outlast Ukraine and eventually wear down the West. If the planned Ukrainian counteroffensive in summer 2023 succeeds, then Russia's strategy will likely have been exposed as a failure, presenting Russia with the set of decisions regarding whether to escalate discussed earlier. The Wagner mutiny highlights internal stability risks that, if they become more acute, could have similar implications. If the Ukrainian counteroffensive falls short of its goals, however, then the question of whether to increase support more rapidly to a Ukrainian military that has likely experienced substantial losses or face the prospect that Russia's strategy of attrition might prove successful in the long run will become more pressing. Essentially, Western leaders could face a decision to either increase the technical capability and lethality of their support to Ukraine in ways that allow Kyiv to achieve a decisive advantage on the battlefield or maintain a more gradual approach to supporting Ukraine that limits at least some escalation risks but leaves open the possibility that Russia may eventually succeed.

---

[4]   David E. Sanger and Steven Erlanger, "Allies Pressure Biden to Hasten NATO Membership for Ukraine," *New York Times*, June 14, 2023.

Fourth, and related to the previous implication, the military capabilities that could be provided to Ukraine that would appear to pose the greatest escalation risks would be those that could enable it to execute long-range strikes against sensitive targets inside Russia, including particularly leadership, command and control, or politically important sites such as Moscow. Although Ukraine may come to perceive either operational or political value in striking such targets, Russia may also view such strikes as posing acute risks to the stability of the regime and be motivated to consider more escalatory measures in response. Such concerns likely informed U.S. hesitation to provide Ukraine with F-16s, despite Ukrainian promises that the aircraft would not be used for such missions. At the other end of the spectrum, however, capabilities with more limited range that would be of use only for attacks on Russian forces inside Ukrainian territory likely present a lower level of escalatory risk.

A fifth implication deals with Russia's ability to modify its war aims. Despite Russia's expansive goals at the outset of its invasion, the Kremlin was initially able to amend these goals in ways that allowed Putin and his inner circle to still claim success in the willingness to abandon attempts to capture Kyiv itself and "denazify" the regime and to instead attempt to illegally annex four provinces in the south and east of Ukraine.[5] However, future Ukrainian successes may not be met with similar Russian adaptability, because Putin's ability to claim success to Russian domestic audiences given the "stake in the ground" that the attempted annexations represent may have narrowed considerably. As a result, his domestic credibility and popularity could decline should further "moving of the goalposts" be attempted, perhaps threatening his hold on power. Under these circumstances, some of the escalation scenarios outlined earlier may become his most viable remaining options for maintaining the initiative and some degree of control.

Sixth, if Russia becomes more desperate and decides to unleash more-destructive attacks against Ukraine's civilian population, an escalatory spiral could develop if Ukraine retaliates by conducting similar attacks, albeit likely at a smaller scale, inside Russia. Recent drone attacks against

---

[5] Treisman, 2022.

Moscow suggest the possibility of a future pattern of escalation in which both sides feel compelled to respond to or go beyond the most recent attacks they have experienced. In this situation, the risks of vertical escalation are clear, but the risks of horizontal escalation against the United States and Europe may also become elevated as Russia gains increasing incentives to reduce Western support for Ukraine or prompt members of the Alliance to pressure Ukraine to cease its attacks. U.S. and NATO policymakers should be prepared to attempt to interrupt such escalation earlier and in a manner that does not undercut Ukrainian battlefield objectives inside Ukraine.

Seventh, Russian internal instability is likely to become an increasingly influential factor in Russian escalation decisions, though the direction of its effects is not yet clear. As the Wagner mutiny highlights, the demands of and losses in the invasion of Ukraine have substantially eroded Russian state capacity, making the Kremlin's control of the country increasingly brittle. However, the effects of this trend on Putin's escalation decisions are likely to be conditional. If the Kremlin believes that the demands of the Ukraine invasion are becoming too great for it to maintain internal order, Russia may be incentivized to reduce resources committed to the conflict and explore possible partial withdrawals or ceasefire arrangements that could give it more time and breathing room for reconstitution. However, faced with the same circumstances, the Kremlin could alternately conclude that, while it lacks the ability to sustain the conflict indefinitely, domestic pressure from right-wing, nationalist sources will not permit it to reduce its commitment to the invasion without having achieved further objectives while still maintaining its hold on power. The Kremlin could then consider further escalatory options that it assesses could shorten the conflict, even at the risk of possible NATO involvement or loss of Chinese support. How Putin will assess these varying risks to regime stability as they become more acute (and, therefore, the effects that they will have on Russian escalation decisions) is difficult to predict in advance.

Finally, although preventing further escalation is likely to remain a key objective of the United States and its allies in the conflict, it is prudent that they should also plan for failure. Efforts to prevent or limit escalation may become increasingly difficult because of external factors that are largely beyond the control of U.S. and European governments. A sudden deterioration in Russian military capability or cohesion inside Ukrainian territory or stability at home are events that Alliance members can do little to control. Ukraine's leaders may also face intense pressure in the future to attack targets inside Russia in retaliation for Russia's increasingly destructive attacks against Ukraine's population and infrastructure, a retaliatory impulse that U.S. policymakers may lack the leverage to fully restrain, even should they attempt to do so. Depending on the trajectory of the conflict, U.S. ability to control future escalation may diminish. This reality makes it necessary for U.S. and allied policymakers to develop their own planning for how to respond to potential further Russian escalatory actions.[6] It also highlights the value and importance of efforts to maintain political and military communication channels with Russia that could become vital to arrest an escalatory spiral. To date, Russia has resisted strengthening such channels, treating them as a concession that could embolden the United States to increase its involvement in the conflict, confident in the knowledge that escalation risks can be more safely managed. Although this perception may be difficult to overcome, U.S. communications with Russia should continue to emphasize the challenges of strengthening such channels on the fly should they become necessary later.

Implications for Future Crises and Conflicts

The examination of Russia's escalatory behavior and future options in Ukraine also provides implications for policymakers as they consider future crises and conflicts, particularly those involving other nuclear-armed states. First, the war in Ukraine makes clear that the ability to control both the outcome of military operations and adversary perceptions thereof, thus finely calibrating and managing potential escalation, is nearly impossible. Although avoiding substantial horizontal escalation (and some forms of vertical escalation) to date is to be welcomed, there have been several factors restraining escalation in this conflict that may not be present elsewhere. Conflicts where U.S. treaty allies are involved directly in combat, where U.S. adversaries may have a more comprehensive set of effective military capabilities, or where the nature of the conflict requires earlier decisions on both

---

[6]   Frederick, Charap, and Mueller, 2022.

sides regarding whether to execute attacks on sensitive targets inside the home territory of their opponents may have substantially greater escalation risks than we have seen to date in Ukraine.

Second, the relatively gradual evolution of the conflict that has likely helped to limit some types of escalation has depended on a very specific set of battlefield conditions. Although Russia's invasion has been deadly and destructive from the start, Russia's failure to achieve its objectives at nearly every turn, paired with Ukraine's gradually built ability to counterattack, has allowed the United States and its allies time to deliberate and gain consensus on the types of support they would provide Ukraine. Similarly, these deliberations played a role in developing a collective approach to risk in which allies eventually arrived at consensus decisions on the type of lethal aid they were willing to provide. In nearly all cases, one ally's willingness to provide a particular system was followed by others that provided similar support. In the end, no ally was left exposed as a singular target for Russian escalation or retaliation, and NATO established and built a pattern and reputation for cohesion and unity. Future scenarios may not provide this same time for collective deliberation. Instead, the pace of developments may be much more rapid, forcing decisions to be made much more quickly. A key question is whether the United States and its allies will be able to make these decisions on the timelines necessary to prevent a future adversary's well-planned and well-coordinated attack from being successful, whether Alliance cohesion could be built and maintained on more compressed timelines, and whether a faster ramp-up in assistance would create greater pressure on an adversary to escalate so as to prevent such assistance from arriving.

Finally, the geographic characteristics of Ukraine that to this point have aided escalation control will likely be different in most future conflicts involving other states. Ukraine is a large country with extensive land borders both with U.S. allies and Russia itself. This fact has meant that U.S. and allied assistance to Ukraine has been relatively easy to provide and relatively difficult to interdict, making Russian strikes on NATO to interdict this support less feasible and therefore less attractive. The distances involved in warfare across Ukraine have provided time: time for the initial Russian attempt to seize Kyiv to be rebuffed, time for Ukraine to gradually rebuild its capabilities, and, later on, time for Russian forces to withdraw and regroup, each of these factors limiting escalation risks by postponing or avoiding critical decision points at which the ultimate fate of the conflict was perceived to be at stake. Ukraine's size, and the amount of Ukrainian territory Russia has controlled from the early days of the war, has also meant that military operations could plausibly be confined inside the territory of Ukraine. In conflicts over smaller pieces of territory, or involving smaller states, military operations would of necessity cross international borders with greater frequency, increasing incentives for cross-border retaliatory or preemptive attacks and likely raising escalation risks. In a future conflict, policymakers will need to carefully assess whether the relatively favorable set of geographic conditions for avoiding escalation in Ukraine are likely to apply.

For all these reasons, the success in avoiding greater escalation to date in the war in Ukraine appears likely to be difficult to repeat in other contexts. If the war in Ukraine does end without substantially greater escalation, this theory should not necessarily hearten policymakers and military planners as they consider the risks that may be involved in other conflicts involving nuclear powers. If greater escalation does ultimately occur in Ukraine despite the factors that have mitigated those risks to date, it would only underscore the risks that are likely in other contexts and the necessity for policymakers to carefully account and plan for those risks in advance of becoming involved in any future conflict with a nuclear-armed adversary.

Abbreviations

CTBT	Comprehensive Test Ban Treaty
EU	European Union
NATO	North Atlantic Treaty Organization
PRC	People's Republic of China
START	Strategic Arms Reduction Treaty
UAS	unmanned aircraft system
VKS	Russian Aerospace Forces

References

Ali, Idrees, and Phil Stewart, "Ukraine Shouldn't Use US Weaponry Inside Russia, US General Says," Reuters, May 25, 2023.

Allison, Graham T., *Essence of Decision: Explaining the Cuban Missile Crisis*, Little, Brown and Company, 1971.

Barnes, Julian E., Adam Entous, Eric Schmitt, and Anton Troianovski, "Ukrainians Were Likely Behind Kremlin Drone Attack, U.S. Officials Say," *New York Times*, May 24, 2023.

Barros, George, Kateryna Stepanenko, Thomas Bergeron, Noel Mikkelsen, and Daniel Mealie, "Interactive Map: Russia's Invasion of Ukraine," Institute for the Study of War and American Enterprise Institute's Critical Threats Project, undated.

Beauchamp, Zack, "Why Is Putin Attacking Ukraine? He Told Us," *Vox*, February 23, 2022.

Bella, Timothy, "Assassination Plot Against Zelensky Foiled and Unit Sent to Kill Him 'Destroyed,' Ukraine Says," *Washington Post*, March 2, 2022.

Belton, Catherine, *Putin's People: How the KGB Took Back Russia and Then Took on the West*, Farrar, Straus and Giroux, 2020.

Betts, Richard K., *Nuclear Blackmail and Nuclear Balance*, Brookings Institution Press, 1987.

"Biden Warns Putin on Use of WMDs: 'Don't, Don't, Don't,'" *Voice of America*, September 17, 2022.

Braithwaite, Alex, and Douglas Lemke, "Unpacking Escalation," *Conflict Management and Peace Science*, Vol. 28, No. 2, April 2011.

Bugos, Shannon, "Russia Further Pauses New START Inspections," *Arms Control Today*, September 2022.

"Chinese Envoy Pledges Efforts to Bring CTBT into Force," Xinhua, September 28, 2021.

Colby, Elbridge A., and Michael S. Gerson, eds., *Strategic Stability: Contending Interpretations*, U.S. Army War College Press, February 2013.

Courtney, William, "Putin Could Escalate with Nuclear Testing," *The Hill*, March 6, 2023.

Diaz-Maurin, François, "Russia Suspends New START and Is Ready to Resume Nuclear Testing," *Bulletin of the Atomic Scientists*, February 21, 2023.

Downs, George W., and David M. Rocke, "Conflict, Agency, and Gambling for Resurrection: The Principal-Agent Problem Goes to War," *American Journal of Political Science*, Vol. 38, No. 2, May 1994, pp. 362–380.

Faiola, Anthony, Fredrick Kunkle, Robyn Dixon, and Catherine Belton, "Putin Rules by Showing Strength. Russia's Crisis Exposed His Weakness," *Washington Post*, June 25, 2023.

Frederick, Bryan, Samuel Charap, and Karl P. Mueller, *Responding to a Limited Russian Attack on NATO During the Ukraine War*, RAND Corporation, PE-A2081-1, December 2022. As of May 10, 2023: https://www.rand.org/pubs/perspectives/PEA2081-1.html

Frederick, Bryan, Matthew Povlock, Stephen Watts, Miranda Priebe, and Edward Geist, *Assessing Russian Reactions to U.S. and NATO Posture Enhancements*, RAND Corporation, RR-1879-AF, 2017. As of May 24, 2023: https://www.rand.org/pubs/research_reports/RR1879.html

Gordon, Chris, "Russian Air Force 'Has Lot of Capability Left' One Year on from Ukraine Invasion," *Air and Space Forces Magazine*, February 15, 2023.

Gottemoeller, Rose, "Russia Is Updating Their Nuclear Weapons: What Does That Mean for the Rest of Us?" Carnegie Endowment for International Peace, January 29, 2020.

Gutiérrez, Pablo, and Ashley Kirk, "A Year of War: How Russian Forces Have Been Pushed Back in Ukraine," *The Guardian*, February 21, 2023.

Higgins, Andrew, and Hana de Goeij, "Czechs Blame 2014 Blasts at Ammunition Depots on Elite Russian Spy Unit," *New York Times*, April 17, 2021.

Hill, Ian, "Russia's Invasion of Ukraine: Why and Why Now?" *The Interpreter*, June 22, 2023.

Kovalev, Alexey, "Putin Has a New Opposition—and It's Furious at Defeat in Ukraine," *Foreign Policy*, September 12, 2022.

Kramer, Andrew E., Michael Schwitz, and Marc Santora, "Ukraine Targets Bases Deep in Russia, Showing Expanded Reach," *New York Times*, December 5, 2022.

Kramer, Andrew E., Valerie Hopkins, and Michael Schwirtz, "Anti-Kremlin Fighters Take War to Russian Territory for a Second Day," *New York Times*, May 23, 2023.

Lieber, Keir A., and Daryl G. Press, *Coercive Nuclear Campaigns in the 21st Century: Understanding Adversary Incentives and Options for Nuclear Escalation*, Project on Advanced Systems and Concepts for Countering Weapons of Mass Destruction, Report No. 2013-001, March 2013.

Lowther, Adam, and Mahbube K. Siddiki, "Combat Drones in Ukraine," *Air and Space Operations Review*, Vol. 1, No. 4, Winter 2022.

Mackinnon, Amy, and Mary Yang, "Ukraine Urges the West to Chill Out," *Foreign Policy*, January 28, 2022.

Masters, Jonathan, and Will Merrow, "How Much Aid Has the U.S. Sent Ukraine? Here Are Six Charts," Council on Foreign Relations, May 19, 2023.

McLaughlin, Elizabeth, and Luis Martinez, "A Look at the US Military's Close Calls with Russia in the Air and at Sea," *ABC News*, April 9, 2020.

Mellen, Riley, "Pro-Ukraine Forces Appear to Have Used U.S.-Made Armored Vehicles in Incursion into Russia," *New York Times*, May 23, 2023.

Meng, Anne, "Accessing the State: Executive Constraints and Credible Commitment in Dictatorship," *Journal of Theoretical Politics*, Vol. 31, No. 4, 2019, pp. 568–599.

Ministry of Foreign Affairs of the People's Republic of China, "China's Position on the Political Settlement of the Ukraine Crisis," February 24, 2023.

Mirovalev, Mansur, "Why Most Ukrainians Don't Believe Biden's Warnings, Distrust West," *Al Jazeera*, February 21, 2022.

Morgan, T. Clifton, and Sally Howard Campbell, "Domestic Structure, Decisional Constraints, and War: So Why Kant Democracies Fight?" *Journal of Conflict Resolution*, Vol. 35, No. 2, June 1991, pp. 187–211.

Morgan, Forrest E., Karl P. Mueller, Evan S. Medeiros, Kevin L. Pollpeter, and Roger Cliff, *Dangerous Thresholds: Managing Escalation in the 21st Century*, RAND Corporation, MG-614-AF, 2008. As of July 14, 2023: https://www.rand.org/pubs/monographs/MG614.html

"Moscow Drone Attack Exposes Russia's Vulnerabilities, Fuels Criticism of Military," Associated Press, May 30, 2023.

Murphy, Matt, "Ukraine War: Russia Accused of Using Phosphorous Bombs in Bakhmut," BBC News, May 6, 2023.

Myers, Steven Lee, *The New Tsar: The Rise and Reign of Vladimir Putin*, reprint ed., Knopf Doubleday Publishing Group, 2016.

North Atlantic Treaty Organization, "NATO's Military Presence in the East of the Alliance," webpage, updated December 21, 2022. As of May 31, 2023: https://www.nato.int/cps/en/natohq/topics_136388.htm

Osborn, Andrew, "Senior Russian Security Official Questions U.S. Commitment to Ukraine After Afghan Exit," Reuters, August 19, 2021.

Pauly, Reid B. C., and Rose McDermott, "The Psychology of Nuclear Brinksmanship," *International Security*, Vol. 47, No. 3, Winter 2022–2023, pp. 9–51.

Posen, Barry R., *Inadvertent Escalation: Conventional War and Nuclear Risks*, Cornell University Press, 1991.

Powell, Robert, "The Theoretical Foundations of Strategic Nuclear Deterrence," *Political Science Quarterly*, Vol. 100, No. 1, Spring 1985, pp. 75–96.

Powell, Robert, "Crisis Stability in the Nuclear Age," *American Political Science Review*, Vol. 83, No. 1, March 1989, pp. 61–76.

Roberts, Brad, "NATO's Nuclear Deterrent: Fit for Purpose?" *SIRIUS Zeitschrift für strategische Analysen*, March 2023. As of July 7, 2023: https://cgsr.llnl.gov/content/assets/docs/Brad-Roberts-english.pdf

Rofer, Cheryl, "Nuclear Tests May Be Back on Moscow's Agenda," *Foreign Policy*, May 15, 2023.

"Russian Mercenary Chief Says He Did Not Intend Coup, Putin Thanks Those Who Stood Down," Reuters, June 26, 2023.

Ryan, Kevin, "Why Putin Will Use Nuclear Weapons in Ukraine," Russia Matters, May 17, 2023.

Sabbagh, Dan, and Luke Harding, "UK Sending Long-Range Storm Shadow Missiles to Ukraine, Says Defence Minister," *The Guardian*, May 11, 2023.

Sagan, Scott D., *The Limits of Safety: Organizations, Accidents, and Nuclear Weapons*, Princeton University Press, 1993.

Sanger, David E., and Steven Erlanger, "Allies Pressure Biden to Hasten NATO Membership for Ukraine," *New York Times*, June 14, 2023.

Schelling, Thomas, *The Strategy of Conflict*, Harvard University Press, 1960.

Schmitt, Eric, "Russian Warplane Hits American Drone over Black Sea, U.S. Says," *New York Times*, March 14, 2023.

Schreck, Adam, "Putin Signs Annexation of Ukrainian Regions as Losses Mount," Associated Press, October 5, 2022.

Sciutto, Jim, "New US Drone Routes Over Black Sea 'Definitely Limit' Intelligence Gathering, Says US Official," CNN, March 28, 2023.

Sechser, Todd S., "Goliath's Curse: Coercive Threats and Asymmetric Power," *International Organization*, Vol. 64, No. 4, Fall 2010, pp. 627–660.

Sechser, Todd S., and Matthew Fuhrmann, "Crisis Bargaining and Nuclear Blackmail," *International Organization*, Vol. 67, No. 1, Winter 2013, pp. 173–195.

Seligman, Lara, "How Biden Got to Yes on F-16s and Ukraine," *Politico*, May 22, 2023.

Siebold, Sabine, and Phil Stewart, "Russian Nuclear Strike Likely to Provoke 'Physical Response,' NATO Official Says," Reuters, October 12, 2022.

Stewart, Phil, and Idrees Ali, "Russia 'Very Unlikely' to Use Nuclear Weapons, US Intel Chief," Reuters, May 4, 2023.

Sukin, Lauren, "Rattling the Nuclear Saber: What Russia's Nuclear Threats Really Mean," Carnegie Endowment for International Peace, May 4, 2023.

Sytas, Andrius, "Estonia Says It Repelled Major Cyber Attack After Removing Soviet Monuments," Reuters, August 18, 2022.

Toosi, Nahal, "The Line Biden Won't Cross on Ukraine," *Politico*, February 23, 2022.

Toosi, Nahal, and Lawrence Ukenye, "Russian Jet's Collision with U.S. Drone Sparks Diplomatic Flurry," *Politico*, March 14, 2023.

Treisman, Rachel, "Putin's Claim of Fighting Against Ukraine 'Neo-Nazis' Distorts History, Scholars Say," NPR, March 1, 2022.

Ven Bruusgaard, Kristin, "How Russia Decides to Go Nuclear," *Foreign Affairs*, February 6, 2023.

Vernon, Will, and Thomas Spender, "Kremlin Drone: Zelensky Denies Ukraine Attacked Putin or Moscow," BBC News, May 3, 2023.

von der Burchard, Hans, "Germany Approves Tank Sales to Ukraine, Bowing to Pressure," *Politico*, April 26, 2022.

Warrick, Joby, "A Legacy of 'Secrecy and Deception': Why Russia Clings to an Outlawed Chemical Arsenal," *Washington Post*, March 19, 2022.